WHAT PEOPLE ARE SAYING ABOUT THE SERIES

An MD Examines

"I enjoyed Does God Still Do Miracles? *and appreciate the amount of work and research that has gone into its preparation."*
—THE LATE DR. PAUL BRAND
SURGEON, MISSIONARY, AND AUTHOR OF *FEARFULLY AND WONDERFULLY MADE*

"Dr. Burke gives medical insight into why many claims of miracles are quite explainable under the realm of science. He presents his evidence in a way that actually builds a case for faith in God and gives answers to some of the toughest questions a doubting mind can have about the sovereignty of God. He gives us a thoughtful examination of our hope in the Great Physician and Healer."
—LORNA DUECK
EXECUTIVE PRODUCER, *LISTEN UP TV*; COMMENTARY WRITER FOR *THE GLOBE AND MAIL*; PRESIDENT, MEDIA VOICE GENERATION

"Dr. Brad Burke's series is an enormously helpful guide for all who yearn for a personal, intimate relationship with God. His critical analysis of personal spirituality is enlightening; his thoughtful answers to some of our toughest questions are both provocative and compelling; his insights into the rising twenty-first-century generation are perceptive; his medical perspective is fascinating; but most of all, his portrayal of the only true God is profound."
—DR. WILLIAM J. McRAE
PRESIDENT EMERITUS, TYNDALE UNIVERSITY COLLEGE AND SEMINARY

"Doctor Brad's pen is sharper than his scalpel. His stories gripped me from page one. His honest search for answers to the mysteries of miracles, suffering, evil, and the existence of God is not just entertaining, it is immensely helpful and practical."
—PHIL CALLAWAY
SPEAKER, AUTHOR OF *LAUGHING MATTERS*

AN M.D. EXAMINES

DOES GOD STILL DO MIRACLES?

DR. BRAD BURKE

Victor®
The Bible Teacher's Teacher

COOK COMMUNICATIONS MINISTRIES
Colorado Springs, Colorado • Paris, Ontario
KINGSWAY COMMUNICATIONS LTD
Eastbourne, England

Victor® is an imprint of
Cook Communications Ministries, Colorado Springs, CO 80918
Cook Communications, Paris, Ontario
Kingsway Communications, Eastbourne, England

DOES GOD STILL DO MIRACLES?
© 2006 by Brad Burke

Published in association with the literary agency of Les Stobbe, 300
Doubleday Road, Tryon, NC 28782.

The Web addresses (URLs) recommended throughout this book are solely
offered as a resource to the reader. The citation of these Web sites does not
in any way imply an endorsement on the part of the author or the publisher,
nor does the author or publisher vouch for their content for the life of this
book.

Cover Design: Marks & Whetstone
Cover Photo Credit: © BigStockPhoto

First Printing, 2006
Printed in the United States of America

1 2 3 4 5 6 7 8 9 10 Printing/Year 10 09 08 07 06

ISBN-13: 978-0-7814-4282-4
ISBN-10: 0-7814-4282-6

LCCN: 2006923055

To my parents, David and Lucille,
who, by God's grace,
instilled within me a passion
for memorization and
meditation on Scripture

*Understanding God, for the
dedicated and faithful believer, is a
day-by-day, hour-by-hour, mind-, heart-,
and soul-grappling journey, yielding
priceless and unfathomable treasures ...
sometimes by the minute ... sometimes
when the saint is least expecting it....*

CONTENTS

ACKNOWLEDGMENTS

My second career as a writer unexpectedly began in my second year of medical school when I stumbled into the creative world of screenwriting. In a sense, An MD Examines came together remarkably like a major Hollywood film, complete with an executive producer, coproducers, editors, directors, a film studio, a screenwriter—even actors and actresses. Using the film analogy, here are the "rolling credits."

I must begin by thanking my Executive Producer on this extensive project, my Lord and heavenly Father. The astonishing way in which God brought all these talented individuals together blows the fuses in my mind. Whether or not this production wins an Oscar here on earth, God, and God alone, deserves all the glory.

Heather Gemmen, my brilliant producer and content editor, rocks! She enthusiastically presented this project to the studio, Cook Communications. My exceedingly wise coproducer, trusted friend, and mentor for more than twenty-five years, Garry Jenkins, helped steer me clear of false doctrine and "fluff."

ACKNOWLEDGMENTS

Craig Bubeck, like an experienced Tinseltown director, finely directed the thematic and visual components of this project at Cook. And the assistant director, Diane Gardner, and film publicist, Michele Tennesen, smoothly coordinated events, meetings, and communiqué between location shoots. There are so many others at Cook who played key roles; I thank them so much for their dedication to spreading God's truth around the world!

Every film needs a good editor. In addition to those mentioned above, Audrey Dorsch worked her own movie magic and brought the scenes together seamlessly.

Script consultants can make or break a film. Several provided valuable advice from scene one to "The End": Garry and Matt Jenkins, Sherri Spence, Dr. Val Jones, Wendy Elaine Nelles, and my parents. God provided other consultants for the production at key times, including world-renowned surgeon and author Dr. Paul Brand.

The Word Guild, the largest Christian writing association in Canada, played the role of a Hollywood talent agency perfectly, bringing together the screenwriter with the editors, producer, script consultant, agent, and even the production company for this powerful movie.

And what's a film without the actors and actresses? My sincere thanks also goes out to all those individuals who brought this film to life by allowing the world to see their inspiring stories.

I am grateful to Les Stobbe, my hardworking agent who helped make this series possible. My heartfelt appreciation also goes to my parents, David and Lucille, whose understanding and support during those tough years when I took a half-decade sabbatical from medicine to write this series ensured my success. I love them both very much.

In almost every film there is a love interest. To Erin, my beautiful wife, I'm looking forward to serving the Lord together for the rest of our lives.

And finally, to my brother Darryl (a stunt coordinator in training) who told me in 1999 that one day I would write a book—and I laughed …

I apologize.

This evil man will come to do the work of Satan with counterfeit power and signs and miracles. He will use every kind of wicked deception to fool those who are on their way to destruction because they refuse to believe the truth that would save them.

—2 THESSALONIANS 2:9–10 NLT

But examine everything carefully; hold fast to that which is good.

—1 THESSALONIANS 5:21 NASB

INTRODUCTION
"IT WAS A MIRACLE!"

The doctors couldn't explain it," the father jubilantly proclaimed. "It was a miracle!"

The pastor nodded as exclamations of "Praise the Lord!" echoed round about me.

With the TV cameras rolling, it was certainly a joyous occasion. A young father and mother, holding their precious one-year-old daughter, stood on the stage of a well-known Southern California church. Several hundred people sat transfixed, listening to the gripping story. I, too, sat in the audience that Sunday morning, convinced by a friend to visit the illustrious church.

According to the parents, their little girl had been born with a "hole in the aorta." The aorta, the largest artery in the body, is a cane-shaped, elastic vessel that moves blood away from the heart. Specialists, administering medications to try to close this "hole," warned the parents that surgery might be necessary. The parents, understandably horrified at the thought, pleaded with the doctors to allow the prayer option first.

The doctors agreed.

DOES GOD STILL DO MIRACLES?

The next day the doctors met with the family. The little girl had not improved, and a scalpel was offered to correct the potentially life-threatening condition. The parents pleaded again with the doctors, this time begging them to recheck this hole.

And so the doctors did. What they found was cause for joyous celebration! The hole had miraculously closed! Surgery was no longer needed, and their daughter made a complete recovery! Smiling in my seat, I was genuinely happy for the parents who were dedicating their little girl to God that morning. To almost everyone in the building and in TV land that day, this was undeniable evidence that a miracle had occurred. Imagine—a hole in the body's largest artery closing without medical intervention!

It certainly seems amazing, doesn't it? But what would you say if I told you that this "hole closing" happens approximately fours times a second, 250 times a minute, 360,000 times a day around the world? If I told you that almost every human alive on this planet had his or her own hole closed indirectly by God, would you still feel inclined to label this healing a miracle?

What you probably don't know, unless you are a medical professional, is that God has cleverly designed our bodies with this hole. Actually, it's not even a hole. It's called a *ductus arteriosus*; a duct that in fetal life connects the aortic arch with the left pulmonary artery. Its purpose is to shunt blood away from the lungs, delivering it instead to the feet and umbilical arteries. When the baby is born, this duct usually constricts, and the blood is delivered instead to the lungs for oxygenation. Occasionally the duct fails to completely close. (Dr. David Connuck, et al., showed that this duct is open in 45 percent of healthy newborn infants in the first sixty hours of life, and it is still open at two to six months of age in 4.5 percent of normal infants.[1]) If the opening is large enough to pose a health threat, indomethacin (a medication) is usually given to the infant to inhibit prostaglandin synthesis and help close it. If this fails, and the condition is serious, surgery is usually necessary.

So the questions naturally arise: Did this little girl's ductus arteriosus close on its own as normally happens? Was it the medications that helped close the duct? Or was it God's supernatural intervention prompted by all the prayers?[2]

INTRODUCTION

We'll never know for sure, will we? Seemingly miraculous healings often don't seem all that miraculous when we understand the mechanical workings of God's greatest handiwork. I could easily fill this book with similar "medical marvels" that you might think are definite miracles, but which in actuality are scientifically studied events with rational explanations.

According to a *Newsweek* poll conducted at the turn of the millennium, "84 percent of adult Americans say they believe that God performs miracles and nearly half (48 percent) report that they have personally experienced or witnessed one."[3] Whether or not you believe God still performs miracles, you would have to agree that we live in a world obsessed with the paranormal. To fill the church pews on a Sunday morning, all a preacher has to do is announce beforehand that his sermon series will focus on miracles, angels, or demons. To empty pews, all he has to do is announce that his sermons will focus on the holiness of God.

But do miracles really show off, to the greatest extent, God's love, power, and dominion?

Well-known Bible teacher Dr. John MacArthur writes:

> In many ways the daily outworking of providence, in which God constantly must orchestrate millions of details and circumstances, is a greater miracle than what we ordinarily think of as a miracle.[4]

The influential people God brings into our lives at opportune moments, the key resources he supplies us with to accomplish his precise goals, his mind-boggling attention to "millions of details and circumstances" to bring about his perfect sovereign plan for our lives—all of this displays God's genius, power, dominion, wisdom, and love much more than "comparatively uncomplicated miracles."[5] Therefore, it is a "greater exercise of faith," insists MacArthur, to believe that God will work everything out by providence, than to believe that God will instantaneously fix our problems with one or two miracles.[6]

Some Christians would disagree, however. The assumed "God miracles" of ordinary tooth fillings and crowns being instantaneously turned into gold during church services and the gold "glory dust" phenomenon whereby God supposedly showers down actual gold glitter on his faithful flock have become all the rage in some churches. Even if God were responsible for these crowd-drawing stunts, would he be all that impressed with his handiwork? I highly doubt it. If people could truly understand the awesomeness of God's providence in their day-to-day lives, they would see just how insignificant such "miracles" are.

No doubt, many of you have been eagerly looking forward to this book in the series. For the sake of space, I've decided to focus attention specifically on *miracles of physical healing.* To better understand why God allows us to suffer, we must first critically examine the subject of miracles. We must ask some key questions: What is a genuine miracle? Is it God's sovereign will that everyone be 100 percent healthy? How exactly does God heal us? Is God still doing miracles of healing today? If so, why isn't he doing more? How common are genuine miracles of healing?

Some, however, might wonder if it's right as Christians to question the origin of the "miracles" allegedly happening all around us. I've spoken with many hurting individuals over the years who have been made to feel like second-rate Christians by friends and relatives because they took seriously Paul's warning to "examine everything *carefully*" (1 Thess. 5:21 NASB). Instead of flat out accepting all the miracle stories we hear every day as the gospel truth, these individuals have carefully studied the Scriptures and closely examined several modern investigative studies on the subject. What has been their reward? They have been criticized, rebuked, humiliated, and made to feel that their faith is full of gaping holes the size of boulders.

Yet I've noticed something very interesting through the years. The same individuals who have taken Paul's admonition to "examine everything *carefully*" in spiritual matters, particularly miracles of physical healing, are often those who have heeded the same words of caution in most areas of life. (I don't think Paul was referring only to doctrinal issues in this verse.) It doesn't matter if it's spectacular testimonials of the paranormal, Internet hoaxes, get-rich-quick schemes, or the exaggerated claims of some alternative medicine "cures" flooding the market, these individuals want to uncover the truth. They don't fall for all the hype and falsehood bombarding our senses every day; they don't let experiences or testimonials dictate what is truth; rather, they carefully examine and reexamine every detail that comes their way. God has blessed these believers with a real love for the truth—*his truth*. They are merely exercising their spiritual gift of prophecy by trying to discern what is of God and what isn't. Doesn't God warn us in the Scriptures that false prophets will come and deceive people with counterfeit signs and wonders (see 2 Thess. 2:9–10)? Why then do Christians in some denominations harshly scold those who are doing what God commands everyone to do?

If you are the type of person who will go to any length to uncover the *real truth* behind a matter, then I want to commend you for your diligence in searching out the truth—no matter how many other Christians will try to put you down in the process. It takes absolutely *no* faith to believe in everything we can see and hear. But it takes real faith and courage to trust in God for what we can't see. For God tells us, "We live by faith, not by sight" (2 Cor. 5:7).

This is, undeniably, a precariously sensitive subject that some churches and authors wouldn't dare touch with a ten-foot Bible. For if we conclude by the end of the book that miracles of healing aren't occurring today, or that they are uncommon, I will have angered many who have based their theology on the idea that God guarantees us health. If, instead, we conclude that miracles are commonplace, and that God wills every believer to be well, I will have offended many dear saints who are suffering terribly with physical sickness. They'll wonder, "If God is doing so many miracles today, why isn't he healing me?"

It is inevitable that I will offend someone in this book. Nonetheless, the apostles never backed down from seeking out and proclaiming the truth—and neither will I.

LOOKING BEFORE WE JUMP

Before we jump with both feet into the heart of this issue, I want to clarify a few things. First of all, I firmly believe that God is still performing miracles of healing today. Second, I firmly believe that we cannot go another step on this all-important journey until we first define a miracle. The term *miracle* has taken on many meanings in our age. World-famous surgeon and author Dr. Paul Brand correctly pointed this out in a personal letter to me:

> The word "miracle" is commonly used amongst Christians as meaning something wonderful that has happened in somebody's life that is attributable to God's answer to their prayers.[7]

Answers to prayers are always wonderful, whether or not they can be explained by natural forces. (Understanding how amazing it is that a "hole in the aorta" can instantly close in a newborn baby might tempt one to term the whole process miraculous!) I want to make it absolutely clear that God can and often does, by his Holy Spirit, in response to prayer, bring about healing in our physical bodies by first healing our spiritual and emotional illnesses. When our Creator helps rid us of our guilt, anger, bitterness, and depression, our physical bodies are allowed to heal.

You must understand, though, that for purposes of discussion, there is an important difference between a *physical miracle* and what some might term a *spiritual miracle*. Both come from God's supernatural power, but a *physical miracle* involves the unexplainable changes in the physical existence and arrangement of molecules—whereas a *spiritual miracle* does not.

I particularly like this scriptural definition of a miracle given by Dr. John MacArthur:

> A miracle is an extraordinary event wrought by God through human agency, an event that cannot be explained by natural forces.[8]

I will demonstrate shortly how this definition is essential to choosing the right paths on our quest into understanding God more.

In this chapter and the chapters to come, I will concentrate mainly on the fleshly aspects of healing. Indeed, spiritual miracles, such as those seen when God saves a person out of sin, happen almost every minute of every day—and often in response to prayer. And they are true miracles because no mortal or natural process can quicken a sinner from death to spiritual life. Yet I will demonstrate in the end with medical studies why it is so important for us to differentiate between a true miracle of *physical healing* and one of *spiritual healing.* Regardless of the differences, prayer is vitally important for healing—spiritual *and* physical. And whether or not a particular healing fits the strict definition of a miracle, *prayer makes a difference!*

If you wish to term any and every answer to your prayer as "miraculous," then by all means do so. In the pages of this book, however, I will use the miracles of Christ and the apostles as a template in carefully examining the "miraculous healings" taking place on the faith-healing circuit today. Millions of people in the church are asking some pretty tough questions about miracles—questions that need to be addressed from Scripture and from a medical standpoint. If you were dying from a rare disease, you would want an experienced medical doctor to carefully examine your body along with every detail of your history, lab reports, and radiological studies to ascertain the truth. In tackling the important topic of miracles, we should be no less thorough in diligently searching out God's truths. For as the apostle Paul strongly encourages us, we need to "examine everything *carefully*" (1 Thess. 5:21 NASB).

Which is precisely what we will do.

DOES GOD STILL DO MIRACLES?

*People of Israel, listen! God publicly
endorsed Jesus of Nazareth by doing
wonderful miracles, wonders, and signs
through him, as you well know.*

—ACTS 2:22 NLT

1

THE GREATEST MIRACLE WORKER

Before we can compare what happened two thousand years ago to what is taking place in faith-healing crusades all around the world, we have to first ask the obvious question: Did the miracles recorded in Scripture actually occur?

Because 84 percent of Americans believe that God performs miracles—and approximately the same percentage believe Christ rose from the dead[1]—it's probably safe to conclude that the majority of Americans accept all or most miracles detailed in the Scripture as truth. To scientists who believe that the laws of nature prove otherwise, Loren Haarsma, a PhD physicist writing in *The World & I*, says, "Scientists can never rule out the possibility that miracles occurred in the past."[2] You can't prove or disprove an ancient miracle in a modern test tube.

As incredible as it may seem, some folks who believe that God had something to do with fashioning the universe also believe that he lacked enough power to pull off any real miracles afterward (known as "hard" deism). That's like believing the gifted Michelangelo painted the famous vaulted ceiling in the Sistine Chapel—but that later he couldn't paint a happy face on the side of a tree!

Because the results of most public-opinion surveys indicate that most of my readers likely accept by faith the existence of an all-powerful and personal God, we won't spend any more time on the question, Did miracles occur? Rather, we will direct our mental energy to the crucial questions: *Why* did the miracles in Scripture occur? What was God's purpose for curing the army general Naaman of leprosy, raising Lazarus from the dead, and making the blind to see? Is this the norm for today?

Studying the Scriptures, you'll notice that miracles, wrought at the hands of God's messengers, were primarily clustered in three brief ages of Bible history, during the lives of

1. Moses and Joshua

2. the prophets Elijah and Elisha

3. Christ and the apostles (after Christ was thirty years of age).

We have no record of healing miracles occurring in large numbers, anywhere, any time, at the hands of just any saint. C. S. Lewis states it plainly: "God does not shake miracles into Nature at random as if from a pepper-caster."[3] Only certain messengers of God were used to perform divine miracles, referred to as "signs and wonders" throughout the Old and New Testament. In 2 Corinthians 12:12 we read, "The things that mark an apostle—signs, wonders and miracles—*were done* among you with great perseverance." Note here that "were" is past tense, and that this verse was written in a time when the apostles were still alive.

Why *were* these signs and wonders performed?

God used these supernatural feats as signs to the people, identifying and authenticating the credentials of his earthly spokesmen. The Gentiles openly responded to the gospel after seeing Paul perform many signs (see Rom. 15:18–19; Mark 16:20; Heb. 2:4). Christ himself did numerous wonders and signs to demonstrate the truth of his message (John 10:24–25; 20:30–31; Acts 2:22). Even in the Old Testament, when Elijah raised from the dead a widow's son, the widow proclaimed, "Now I know that you are a man of God and that the word of the LORD from your mouth is the truth" (1 Kings 17:24). With the canon of Scripture incomplete, and with so many false prophets buzzing around, citizens had difficulty separating God's truth from human imagination. But by orchestrating an inexplicable, miraculous event through his prophet, or apostle, or his own Son, God effectively channeled his truth to the people.

To accomplish this, God performed miraculous healings that blew away the magic, trickery, and psychosomatic healings of his competition—namely Satan and the false prophets. If you examine Christ's healing ministry in detail, you'll see exactly what I mean.

When Christ instantaneously healed a paralytic, lowered through the roof, the people praised God, declaring, "We have never seen anything like this!" (Mark 2:12). No wonder. I've cared for many paralyzed patients, some on ventilators completely paralyzed from the neck down, and never once have I seen anyone suddenly get up and start walking around. (Nor have I ever seen or heard of a faith healer walking into a hospital and healing such a patient.)

In spinal-cord paralysis, the impulses from the brain that normally inhibit a muscle from firing are lost—resulting in disfiguring and debilitating muscle, ligament, and tendon contractures (shortenings) that can be remedied only by surgery, medications, botox or phenol injections, and/or hours of intensive rehabilitation. Even if the paralytic whom Christ healed didn't have an irreparable spinal-cord lesion or an incapacitating muscle or nerve disorder, he would still require weeks of rehab to overcome the debilitating muscular wasting. Either way, this healing is without a medical explanation—it's supernatural, above nature.

When Christ restored the sight of a man born blind, the Pharisees couldn't explain it (John 9:1–34). You see, a child's brain, part of the central nervous system, continues to lay down structural neuronal pathways till at least age two. If you cover an infant's eye with a patch for too long, the brain never recovers, resulting in permanent blindness in that eye. For an adult born blind to fully regain sight, these undeveloped parts of the brain, particularly the occipital cortex, would have to instantaneously and completely regenerate. Here too was another healing without medical explanation.

DOES GOD STILL DO MIRACLES?

In addition, Christ immediately healed a man of leprosy (Matt. 8:1–4). Admittedly, the term *leprosy* in the New Testament probably described many skin conditions, so this man may have had leprosy as we know it today or he may have been suffering from a disease such as chronic psoriasis. Jesus healed crowds of people, and no doubt one or more had true leprosy. Victims of this cruel disease usually have skin nodules, plaques, and/or rashes. Because of peripheral nerve involvement, leprosy patients gradually lose feeling in their limbs and skin appendages, causing them to be broken, worn off, torn off, or badly ulcerated. Instantaneously healing such bodies would be miraculous. Even if what the healed individual had was your garden-variety chronic psoriasis and it disappeared instantly, that would still be a miracle. Again, this healing defied all medical explanation.

Perhaps Christ's greatest miracle was seen in raising Lazarus from the grave (John 11:11–44). When the brain in a warm environment is deprived of oxygen for more than three or four minutes, there is often irreversible brain damage. (In extremely cold environments the brain can go without oxygen for much longer time periods before damage occurs. That's why you sometimes hear of individuals falling through the ice and being pulled out and resuscitated twenty minutes later with few—or no—adverse effects.) Scientists are scrambling to figure out how to regenerate cells in an adult's central nervous system—but so far without success. For Lazarus, dead for three days in a warm tomb, to be raised to complete health was truly beyond medical rationalization. And Christ raised not one, but at least two other individuals to life—one right out of a coffin on the way to his funeral (Luke 7:14–15; 8:49–56)!

Christ's miracles of healing had these distinctive characteristics:

1. *Christ healed completely:* Christ had no half cures. The paralytic didn't hobble away; the leper didn't go back to the priest with only a few skin nodules here and there; and the blind man didn't need glasses or a seeing-eye camel to find his way around.

2. *Christ healed immediately:* Except for three instances, where the healing took place in a matter of minutes, all

miracles happened instantaneously—not days or weeks later.

3. *Christ healed in public:* His healing ministry was not limited to certain prearranged sites. He didn't need an emotionally supercharged atmosphere or an "anointing" in a crusade or church to heal the sick. He went up and down the countryside and streets healing people in a seemingly random manner. (Of course, he foreknew exactly whom he would heal.)

4. *Christ healed mostly visible organic disease:* He was not intimidated by withered body parts, the blind, or people in the grave. His miracles were so convincing that not even his critics of the day could refute them.

5. *Christ healed even those without faith:* Christ healed without partiality, healing even those who apparently had little or no faith. You'll remember that the man Christ healed of blindness didn't even really know who Christ was. "He replied, 'Whether [Christ] is a sinner or not, I don't know. One thing I do know. I was blind but now I see!'" (John 9:25; see also vv. 35–36).

6. *Christ healed with a purpose:* His purpose was to authenticate his messianic claim (John 5:36), to show the people that he had the authority to forgive sins (Matt. 9:6), to prove that his message came from God (Acts 2:22), and through it all to launch the beginning of his church and bring more glory to God (Eph. 2:19–22; John 11:4). Christ didn't heal everyone (John 5:3–5); nor did he heal on demand (Matt. 12:38–40).

Christ healed without bias—any type of person, anywhere, instantaneously, totally, any disease, in plain sight of everyone. The disciples' healings followed suit. Peter and Paul completely healed the lame (Acts 3:7; 14:8–10), and both apostles raised the dead (Acts 9:40; 20:9–12).

DOES GOD STILL DO MIRACLES?

The apostles' healings were so numerous and so convincing that not even their enemies could deny them (Acts 4:15–17).

But as Dr. John MacArthur points out, after Pentecost (the birth of the church), "no miracle ever occurred in the entire New Testament record except in the presence of an apostle or one directly commissioned by an apostle."[4] Like Christ, the apostles didn't perform miracles simply for the physical benefit of the recipients. Miracles were never intended to make all believers healthy or to be a last-ditch effort by God to bring a person to saving faith. (A miracle by itself will *never* bring someone to genuine faith in God [see John 6:65].) Neither is there evidence in Scripture that the miracles performed by the apostles were to continue after they died. Miracles of healing had a very specific purpose: to authenticate the apostles (2 Cor. 12:11–12) and their message from God, and therein build the foundation for the church (Eph. 2:19–22)—the spiritual framework supporting the very life of the body of genuine believers.

Neither were miracles performed for the *sole reason* that Christ had compassion on the people. On a few occasions in the gospels it specifically says that Christ had "compassion" and healed the sick. But didn't Christ have compassion on the sick when he was twenty-one? Didn't he see people suffer terribly right before his eyes when he was twenty-five? Did he just stand there and watch these people suffer horrible diseases like leprosy and cancer when he had the power to cure them?

We read in the Bible that Christ performed his first miracle at Cana when he turned the water into wine (John 2:1–11). After studying carefully the first couple chapters in Luke and John, we can deduce that Christ's first miracle occurred shortly *after* he started his ministry at approximately thirty years of age.[5] So why did Christ wait until he was about thirty to miraculously heal people and display to the world his miracle-working powers? *Because Christ healed with a purpose.* And that purpose was achieved in a predetermined period two thousand years ago. This is just further evidence that God (in this case, God the Son) works differently in different periods of time, as evidenced all the way through the Scriptures from Genesis to Revelation.

And here is just another example of God's wise parenting strategies.

Miracles had a specific purpose for the church; but as adults today we don't need signs and wonders to authenticate the words of God's ambassadors; we already have God's Word written down for us in black and white. Nor do we need spectacular healings to prove to the unsaved that God exists. Remember what Abraham said when the rich man in Hades begged the patriarch to send Lazarus back from the grave to warn his brothers: "He said to him, 'If they do not listen to Moses and the Prophets, they will not be convinced even if someone rises from the dead'" (Luke 16:31). If the unsaved will not believe what the written Word of God says and apply it in their lives, no miracle will ever convince them. The unbeliever may stick around in the church to see more spectacular "healings," but a genuine miracle by itself will *never* bring anyone to completely surrender his or her life to God.

Many of you have probably heard the story of Ryan Corbin, Pat Boone's grandson. One day in June 2001, while sun tanning on the roof of an apartment Ryan somehow fell through a skylight, falling forty feet to the floor below. He suffered a severe head injury, and in the beginning the doctors didn't think he would live. But he did, although he was left severely disabled, in a wheelchair and unable to walk on his own.

After the accident the family was interviewed four times on *Larry King Live*. In an April 2003 interview for Billy Graham's *Decision* magazine, Pat Boone said this:

> Larry King himself acknowledges that he's an agnostic.
>
> … Larry views it, I think, as a test case. He's looking to see what God does in Ryan's case. Perhaps he is thinking, "Is God going to hear your prayer? What is your faith based on? Why do you think prayer makes a difference?"
>
> … Ryan, I'm confident, is going to walk into Larry King's studio one day and share what God has done. I pray that God will allow me to be there with Ryan and say, "Larry, has God shown you what you needed to see? Do you doubt that God has done this for Ryan?" I would like to hear him saying, "No, I don't doubt it. There is no other explanation. It is miraculous."[6]

DOES GOD STILL DO MIRACLES?

Pat Boone, like so many others, believes that agnostics like Larry King will automatically believe in God and put their faith in him if they can only see a miracle: "Larry, has God shown you what you needed to see?" But, folks, this isn't the issue in an unrepentant heart. Even the demons *know* with 100 percent certainty that a personal and powerful God exists. They have seen firsthand the miracles of God. And they tremble (James 2:19)! But they will never submit their lives to God in worship and complete surrender. Why? Because the limiting factor in conversion is not belief that God exists, but rather submission to the lordship of Christ. And no number of miracles can accomplish this feat without humble submissiveness in a person's life, made possible only by the inward drawing of the Holy Spirit (John 6:44; Eph. 2:1–10).

The influential German philosopher Friedrich Nietzsche said, "If you could prove God to me, I would believe Him all the less."[7] It wouldn't matter if Ryan died, was buried, and rose to life a week later—no miracle is ever going to change Larry King until he is ready to submit his life to God. Larry King has interviewed numerous Christians with amazing inspirational stories of God's powerful working—yet he remains an agnostic. Genuine conversion takes place primarily in the heart—not in the brain, and not in the eyes.

Even in the New Testament, miracles were never intended to bring masses of people to a saving faith. Though numerous miracles authenticated the ministry of Christ and his apostles, and established a recognizable launch of a new divine parenting strategy era, the mind-boggling miracles did not produce widespread faith (see Luke 10:13–15). The masses still crucified Christ and murdered his disciples.

Using Scripture as our model, we arrive then at the definition I gave earlier of signs and wonders—genuine miracles of healing.

> A *miracle* is an extraordinary event wrought by God through human agency, an event that cannot be explained by natural forces.[8]

With this definition in hand, let's carefully compare what is taking place in modern faith-healing circles to what Christ and the apostles did two thousand years ago.

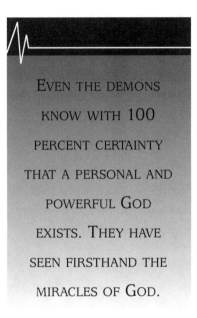

EVEN THE DEMONS
KNOW WITH 100
PERCENT CERTAINTY
THAT A PERSONAL AND
POWERFUL GOD
EXISTS. THEY HAVE
SEEN FIRSTHAND THE
MIRACLES OF GOD.

*Many will say to me on that day,
"Lord, Lord, did we not prophesy in your
name, and in your name drive out
demons and perform many miracles?" Then
I will tell them plainly, "I never knew
you. Away from me, you evildoers!"*

—MATTHEW 7:22–23

2
FAITH HEALERS: GOD'S SERVANTS OR GOD'S EMBARRASSMENTS?

A woman in Uganda, acting as a "messenger of the Virgin Mary," attracted thousands of AIDS patients to her doorstep by claiming she could miraculously cure AIDS with holy soil. Scientists later exposed this not-so-holy soil as being "ordinary dirt."[1]

Faith healer Peter Popoff amazed millions with his "miraculous" ability to "call out" people and heal them—until magician and hoax debunker James Randi exposed Popoff's trickery on the *Tonight Show* in February 1986. Popoff's wife, Elizabeth, collected people's information beforehand and fed it to her husband during the healing services via a hearing device concealed in his ear. She even relayed which wheelchairs were "rentals," guaranteeing Popoff that the person could get up and walk if asked to do so.[2] (Individuals who walk in to a faith service feeling very fatigued are often given rental wheelchairs for the evening. Those who walk in to receive a wheelchair always walk out.[3])

DOES GOD STILL DO MIRACLES?

CBS-TV's *West 57* exposed a similar wheelchair trick used by the faith healer W. V. Grant.[4] In addition, Randi, in his book *The Faith Healers*, published photographs revealing Grant's tricks in making it appear as though he were lengthening legs.[5] Grant was also caught speaking softly on stage to those "miraculously" cured of blindness, informing them how many fingers he was holding up. The audience falsely believed those "healed" of blindness had regained perfect vision.[6]

The sick still travel in masses to the Philippines to be "miraculously" healed by "psychic surgeons" who claim to be able to remove tumors, appendixes, and demon-possessed tissue, through the power of Christ, without making an incision. This, despite the fact that Dr. William A. Nolen, MD, and others have personally witnessed and documented these charlatans palming animal parts and pulling off other sleight-of-hand tricks to fool patients.[7]

Joe Nickell, magician and author of several compelling books demystifying the paranormal, stresses, "There are infinite ways to fake anything."[8] It is extremely easy to be fooled by personal experiences. Peter Popoff, W. V. Grant, "psychic surgeons," and the world's leading magicians can easily fool our senses in numerous ways as demonstrated.

But can faith healers even fool themselves?

Listen to Jesus' warning in Matthew's gospel:

> Many will say to me on that day, "Lord, Lord, did we not prophesy in your name, and in your name drive out demons and perform many miracles?" Then I will tell them plainly, "I never knew you. Away from me, you evildoers!" (Matt. 7:22–23)

Notice something very interesting here: Christ never acknowledged that these "supernatural feats" of prophesying, driving out demons, and performing miracles actually took place. Christ just says, "I never knew you. Away from me, you evildoers." For centuries now, we have interpreted these verses to mean that even an unbeliever can perform all these amazing signs and wonders.[9] Is it possible, though, that these signs and wonders mentioned here never even took place? (I don't believe they were lying to Christ, either.) Therefore, if even the "miracle worker" performing the "miracle" can be fooled into thinking that such spectacular healings are genuine miracles, how much more can the spectator be fooled?

It amazes me how many people readily admit to the great power of Satan, labeled the Angel of Light, while still believing, without question, that absolutely every merit-worthy thought, idea, vision, dream, healing, and revelation that comes their way is from God. Though the majority of faith healers may not be frauds and tricksters, it's imperative that we examine carefully the claims of those individuals healing in the name of God. We must avoid being fooled by our senses at all costs!

The successful American surgeon, Dr. Nolen, who operated on more than fifty-six hundred patients, took on this monumental task. In his definitive book, *Healing: A Doctor in Search of a Miracle*, Nolen set out with an open mind to examine the miraculous healing claims of the most famous healers—including the flamboyant Kathryn Kuhlman, heralded by many charismatics as the greatest faith healer of the twentieth century. Several prominent faith healers, such as Benny Hinn, have extolled Kuhlman as being a great inspiration and influence to their own healing ministries. In fact, Hinn has confessed to frequenting Kuhlman's grave site to acquire the "anointing" from her bones.[10]

To see the healings firsthand, Dr. Nolen volunteered his services as an usher at one of Kulhman's miracle services. Arriving early, he watched in sadness as the sick entered the auditorium. There were drooling, paralyzed stroke victims; crippled children, arms and legs withered; some mentally handicapped. Parents carried or wheeled in children suffering from birth defects, hydrocephalus, and chorea. Almost every person, said Nolen, "had the desperate look of those who have all but given up."[11]

All the ushers were gathered and given strict instructions by Kuhlman's aide: "Those of you who are in the wheelchair section have a big job. No one is supposed to go to the stage unless they have been healed."[12] (A twenty-one-year-old man, claiming a cure from his liver disease, was denied access to the stage because his distended, "tumor-laden" abdomen said otherwise.)[13] Scores of people, however, claiming cures of cancer, arthritis, acne, and multiple sclerosis, paraded up on stage, drawing cheers from the audience.

At one point, Kuhlman called out for someone in particular who no longer needed a brace. A twenty-year-old girl with polio limped onto the stage. Dr. Nolen later wrote, "She waved her leg brace in the air and stood, with her pelvis tilted badly, on one good leg and one short, withered leg." She cried for joy as everyone in the auditorium applauded. The whole scene, said Nolen, was "utterly revolting."[14]

He went on to say,

> [The girl's leg] was just as withered now as it had been ten minutes earlier, before Kathryn Kuhlman called for someone to remove her brace. Now she stood in front of ten thousand people giving praise to the Lord—and indirectly to Kathryn Kuhlman—for a cure that hadn't occurred and wasn't going to occur. I could imagine how she'd feel the next morning, or even an hour later, when the hysteria of the moment had left her and she'd have to again put on the brace that had been her constant companion for thirteen years and would be with her the rest of her life.[15]

After the service, Nolen observed, "All the desperately ill patients who had been in wheelchairs were still in wheelchairs"—even some of those who had claimed cures on stage. Nolen watched the "hopeless cases leave, seeing the tears of the parents as they pushed their crippled children to the elevators."[16] "Not once, in the hour and a half that Kathryn Kuhlman spent healing," wrote Dr. Nolen, "did I see a patient with an obvious organic disease healed (i.e., a disease in which there is a structural alteration)."[17]

But Nolen didn't give up. He had legal secretaries in the audience approach those "cured" after they exited the stage, collecting as many addresses as they could. Nolen ended up with eighty-two names.[18] All were sent letters, but only twenty-three showed up to be interviewed.

After investigating every case, Dr. Nolen came away still in search of a miracle.

I will list the five typical cases Nolen documented because these reported "healings" are similar to many seen in the typical faith-healing service today:[19]

Case #1—An eighteen-year-old woman, Marilyn, with multiple sclerosis, feeling fatigued and dizzy, borrowed a wheelchair the night of the miracle service. Feeling a "burning sensation" in her spine, Marilyn deserted her wheelchair and ambled to the stage. Kuhlman praised God for healing this young woman, giving her the amazing ability to walk. But as Nolen observed later in the interview, "To my eye, there was no discernible improvement in Marilyn's gait. But I was glad her spirits were so high."[20]

Case #2—A twenty-two-year-old man in the choir reluctantly stood up, acknowledging that God had instantly cured his migraines. He later confessed to Dr. Nolen that he still suffered from migraines, but possibly they were a little better.[21]

Case #3—A fifty-three-year-old Roman Catholic nun stood on stage waving her arm high—supposedly cured from "a sort of bursitis," as her doctor put it. She confessed later to Dr. Nolen that she still had problems with her shoulder, but felt there was maybe some improvement.[22]

Case #4—Kuhlman called out a twenty-three-year-old woman with acne: "Someone there—someone in Section Six—is suffering from a skin problem. I rebuke that problem. In three days that skin problem will be cured." Upon examination later, Nolen admitted there was some improvement in the woman's acne, but noted that "the scars, an organic manifestation of the disease," still remained.[23]

Case #5—A thirty-six-year-old woman with troublesome varicose veins was healed—despite the fact that no one, including the woman herself, could clearly see her legs (she was wearing panty-hose and a pantsuit). Her varicose veins did improve, but what she didn't tell anyone was that she had just delivered a baby two months earlier. Varicose veins, a common disorder in pregnancy, subside and usually disappear in the months following delivery.[24]

Dr. Nolen also followed up with patients who claimed cures at Kuhlman's services from malignant diseases.

- The twenty-one-year-old young man, denied access to the stage, died twelve days later of his abdominal cancer.[25]

- A sixty-three-year-old man, for whom Dr. Nolen had provided a temporary wheelchair at the event, falsely answered yes when Kuhlman asked if it was his wheelchair. Because the man could perform deep-knee bends on stage, Kuhlman praised God for healing the man's kidney cancer. He felt well for three or four days, but X-rays soon afterward revealed the tumor was even larger.[26]

- A sixty-seven-year-old man with prostate cancer who praised God on stage for a cure still had the cancer afterward.[27]

- A woman, supposedly cured of cancer that had spread to her bone, took off her back brace and danced around the stage. At four the next morning she awoke in excruciating pain. X-rays showed partially collapsed vertebrae that her doctor attributed to her on-stage acrobatics. The brace went back on. Four months later, she died from the cancer.[28]

- Another woman, up on stage, who claimed healing of "lung cancer," was asked by Kuhlman to take a deep breath. The woman did—painlessly. "Do you see her?" Kuhlman shouted to the audience, "Lung cancer. And now she can breathe without pain. The Holy Spirit is surely working here today." What Kuhlman didn't know was that a few painless breaths can't prove a cure from lung cancer. What Kuhlman also didn't know (but the Holy Spirit did) was that the woman didn't even have lung cancer—she had Hodgkin's lymphoma. She later admitted, "I never had much trouble with my breathing anyway." What's more, she wasn't cured. The Hodgkin's lymphoma was still there.[29]

At Dr. Nolen's request, Kuhlman sent him a letter listing the cases of sixteen patients she had "cured" with a miracle.[30] Dr. Nolen noticed instantly that "two thirds of the patients suffered from diseases ... in all of which the psyche often plays a major and dominant role. It was apparent from her letter that Miss Kuhlman knew very little—next to nothing—about psychosomatic diseases."[31] Again, upon further investigation of the cases, no miracle was uncovered.[32]

Dr. Nolen, who believes in the existence of God, took seriously the mandate to "examine everything *carefully*."

"After doing my very best for eighteen months," wrote Dr. Nolen, "to find some shred of evidence that somewhere there was someone who had miraculous healing powers, I concluded that no such person existed."[33]

BENNY HINN

Without question, the most prominent faith healer on the planet today is Benny Hinn. Millions of people cram his miracle crusades every year, and millions more watch his television show around the world. Over the years, several documentary programs have carefully investigated Hinn's ministry and his healing services.

In the early 1990s the TV show *Inside Edition* planted a hired actress at a Benny Hinn crusade. (Hinn's ministry officials report that about one thousand people at each crusade are miraculously healed.) This actress, who faked healing of cerebral palsy, was displayed on stage and her "cure" hailed an undeniable miracle by Hinn. In his defense, Hinn has confessed to getting his wires crossed from the Holy Spirit occasionally.[34]

In September 1992, Hinn forwarded three medical cases to Hank Hanegraaff's *Christian Research Institute* as proof of his miracle-working abilities. Hanegraaff promptly turned the documents over to a medical consultant, Dr. Preston Simpson, who described the cases as "poorly documented and confused."[35] In one case the pathology report read, "no evidence of malignancy." But closer inspection of the report revealed that the colon tumor had been "surgically removed"—not "miraculously cured" by Hinn. The second case involved the supposed remission of a patient's lupus. Lupus is a chronic and relapsing multisystem disease that often goes into remission—sometimes for years. (In this case, however, the effects of the lupus were still visible in the sacroiliac joint of the pelvis.) And the third case revealed a spinal tumor that started shrinking three months before Hinn's crusade—but was "still present—not healed" months after the crusade.[36]

"Miracles are going to happen all over the place!"[37] cries Hinn at some of his crusades. Yet these were apparently the three best cases Hinn could produce from his thousands of testified healings. With so many TV cameras at these miracle crusades, one would think they should be able to capture at least one instantaneous and highly visible healing of someone being cured from leprosy or complete spinal-cord paralysis. If Dr. Nolen visited Hinn's crusades, would he uncover the same dismal results he did with Kuhlman?[38]

In April 2001, HBO aired the *America Undercover* episode "A Question of Miracles," in which the producers vigilantly investigated Hinn's claims. Hinn supposedly performed seventy-six miracles on stage one night in Portland, Oregon, but could produce only five cases as "proof" to HBO thirteen weeks later. When the cases were carefully investigated, not one was found to be a miracle. That same evening, ten-year-old Ashnil Prakash was brought to Hinn for cure from a brain tumor. "Although his impoverished parents pledge thousands of dollars to Hinn," the producers reported, "Prakash died seven weeks after the Portland event."[39]

Yet this hasn't stopped Benny Hinn, and scores of others, from making outlandish, unsupported claims of the miraculous. Hinn once boasted,

> You know we had a lady in service that came with a pace-maker and God burnt that thing out of her body they could

not even, they could not find the pacemaker, they opened her up and the thing was gone out of her body.[40]

Predictably, proof of the miracle never surfaced. Hinn once claimed that a man rose from the dead at his Ghana crusade. He said this on TV at one of his crusades: "I was in Ghana just recently. We had half a million people show up. And a man was raised from the dead on the platform. That's a fact, people. We had it on video."[41] But it was all a lie. When later pressed, Hinn confessed that he never actually saw or possessed the videotape.[42]

To be fair and thorough, I thought I should follow in Dr. Nolen's footsteps and attend a healing crusade of a famous faith healer just to see for myself what is going on in the "name of God." So on August 19, 2004, I attended a Benny Hinn "miracle service" held in the Air Canada Centre in Toronto, Ontario. Hinn packed out the stadium three times in a twenty-four-hour period. He seemed comfortable back on his home turf. As a teenager he had attended a high school just north of Toronto.

I arrived two hours early to find a seat, as I knew the approximately twenty-thousand-seat stadium would be packed out well before Hinn even stepped on the platform. I found a seat just up from the corner of the stage, where I had a clear view of everything going on. I shook hands with the friendly guy beside me, David, a bright young man with an infectious zeal for Christ. He was married with a couple of children, and had just moved from Nigeria to Canada three years before.

I brought my binoculars, but I was close enough that I didn't really need them. In the section just below me, I noticed that the last row had been reserved for a line of people in wheelchairs. Most of the wheelchairs these individuals were seated in appeared to be their own—not the generic or rental wheelchairs that I had observed being offered to those who had walked in feeling weak and fatigued.

About an hour before the service started, I noticed a man, probably in his forties, a little on the heavy side, moving along the floor in his customized electric wheelchair toward the front of the stage. He stopped at the corner closest to me and just sat there. He appeared determined to be as close as possible to all the action.

DOES GOD STILL DO MIRACLES?

Was he expecting a healing that evening?

It wasn't long before a couple of ushers came over and pointed to the back, apparently asking him to return to the rear of the stadium. After a short discussion, the man reluctantly turned his wheelchair around and headed off.

About fifteen minutes before the service was scheduled to begin, the same man in the electric wheelchair returned. It was obvious that this time he wasn't going to budge so easily. The ushers tried and tried but could not convince the man to move. Losing patience, one usher tried pushing buttons on the wheelchair's control box in an attempt to move it himself. But either he was pushing the wrong buttons or the owner had the controls in locked mode, and the heavy chair wasn't going anywhere. Having had enough, the two ushers seized the wheelchair and pushed and pulled as hard as they could, skidding the man in his bulky black chair along the smooth concrete floor toward the back. After about six or eight feet of this tug of war, the disabled man admitted defeat. He put the wheelchair in drive and took off again to the back of the stadium.

I realize that, for the sake of order and security, people may not be allowed to park their wheelchairs just anywhere in a faith-healing service. But as I was watching all this unfold, I wondered to myself what Christ and his apostles would have done in a similar situation? Would the apostles have done like Hinn's ushers and forcibly pushed one of the most disabled individuals to the back of the crowd so that some of the healthiest, best dressed, and most prominent donors and friends could maintain their front-row seats?[43]

Remember the demon-possessed slave girl who followed Paul and others around like a lost puppy, shouting, "These men are servants of the Most High God, who are telling you the way to be saved?" (Acts 16:17). Finally, after enduring days of this annoying woman hollering in his ear, Paul got fed up and drove out the demon. Had Paul been present that night at Hinn's crusade, what would he have done with this determined man in the electric wheelchair? Would Paul have pushed the man to the back? Or would he have healed the gentleman right there on the spot? "You want to be healed, do you? Then I'll heal you! There, now you can sit, stand, run, jump, do cartwheels—go wherever you want!"

I couldn't help but wonder, why didn't someone out of twenty thousand or so people in attendance come forward and heal this man in his electric wheelchair? I'm sure all he wanted was a healing.

As this was a "miracle service," shouldn't Hinn's ushers have gathered up the most critically ill and disabled individuals and sat them directly in front of the stage? Why were the sickest individuals pushed toward the back or seated in the back rows of certain sections? The reason Hinn probably doesn't seat the sickest people in front is because, as at Kathryn Kuhlman's crusades, the sickest and most disabled individuals leave the crusades without a healing. Imagine watching a "healing crusade" where people were getting up on stage claiming cures from arthritis, fibromyalgia, and asthma, when twenty feet away there were rows of ailing people who were totally blind from birth, or in wheelchairs suffering debilitating joint contractures from cerebral palsy, or completely paralyzed from the waist or neck down—some on ventilators. It wouldn't look very good for the famous faith healer, would it?

The man in the electric wheelchair never returned to the front, and the service began without incident shortly after 7:00 p.m. I have to admit that I liked the next hour and a half. The singing was excellent, with special singers and the choir and crowd singing such songs as "Majesty" and "How Great Thou Art." Benny gave an excellent gospel message, using several key Scripture verses to clearly preach on sin, hell, the depravity of man, and what Christ accomplished on the cross. I thought, *Wow, this is great!*

Then came the amazing testimonies of physical healing. I could see the excitement and wonder building on David's face with every story. A pastor from India went on stage and told about one woman with a "tumor in the stomach." Apparently she shunned medical attention, preferring instead to be prayed over and the "tumor fell off the body." She then picked it up and put "the tumor in a plastic bag."

Many other testimonials were given, all just as remarkable.

At the two-hour mark, Hinn announced loudly, "The power of God is going to hit this place like a Holy Ghost hurricane!" and, you will get "drunk in the Holy Ghost!" In regard to physical miracles, Hinn said, "Tonight is your night. Expect it. Don't let anyone steal it." Each time he unleashed such a line, the massive congregation in the stadium erupted into cheers. David, eyes closed, his hands lifted toward heaven, was seemingly praising God with words I couldn't understand.

Then, listing many of the miracles Christ had performed, Hinn declared that Christ is still healing today because, "Jesus Christ is the same yesterday and today and forever" (Heb. 13:8). "He healed them then, he'll heal them today. He hasn't changed…. He is still Jesus," declared Hinn.

"Praise Jesus!" exclaimed David.

At about the three-hour mark, the repetitious choruses began with the massive choir (almost filling the entire section of seats directly behind the stage) singing over and over again such phrases as, "Jesus, oh Jesus," "Rise and be healed," and "You do miracles so great." The music played softly in the background and the colored lights dimmed. The more the choir sang, the more empty wheelchairs the ushers brought forward to the front of the stage. I counted at least seven TV cameras rolling at that point.

"Lift your hands and receive your miracle from the Master!" shouted Hinn. Things were getting a bit eerie, however. People were shaking, crying, and chanting. David seemed to be going into a trance, speaking in tongues—as was another young man swaying below me who I thought was about to fall forward into the next row of people. One young, muscular black guy, dressed casually in a bright polo shirt, a few rows down from me was literally howling. A woman, (I think it was a woman) several sections away, was screeching—I was surprised I could hear her from that distance. Minutes later, people started dropping like flies on and off the stage, a practice known as being "slain in the Spirit," in which the Holy Spirit supposedly falls with such power on people that they are "slain."

The music was getting louder and louder. So was the shouting and clapping. "Believe him now for your healing!" Hinn yelled. He was working the crowd into a near-hysterical state of wonderment and euphoria unlike anything I'd ever seen before. "I rebuke your sickness in Jesus' name!" he thundered. "Heart disease is cured in the back! Cancer there! Arthritis there!" He was pointing and calling out all kinds of diseases.

"There's a mighty wind of healing going through this place!" he bellowed. David and most of the crowd cheered even louder.

Then those "healed" started coming forward. The ushers appeared to be selecting certain ones and moving them to the front of the lines on each side of the stage. The wheelchairs were placed (some tossed) onto the stage. One by one, Hinn's staff brought to the platform those who had been healed.

Looking at the last row of the section below me, I noticed that most, if not all, of the disabled who were sitting in a row of wheelchairs at the beginning of the service were still there. They had not been healed. I also noticed that many—if not all—of the empty wheelchairs on the stage were the generic ones offered to those who walked in off the street.

Every time Benny Hinn welcomed someone healed onto the stage, I wrote down the disease he announced. The "healings" included cures from Hodgkin's disease, breast cancer, "skin disease," metastatic cancer, heart disease, chronic fatigue, pulmonary fibrosis, lymphoma, fibromyalgia, arthritis, diabetes, leukemia, liver cancer, asthma, back pain, cervical cancer, herniated disk, and tendinitis (somewhere in the ankle or foot). These diseases were very similar to the ones Dr. Nolen heard at Kathryn Kuhlman's crusade. And just as Dr. Nolen observed, all of this "healing" involved diseases that no one could easily see. Several of those healed claimed they had more strength, or no pain, or that they didn't need their oxygen anymore.

Only one case that evening might have displayed visible results. A French-speaking woman walked on stage with a friend who could speak some English. She pronounced a disease that sounded like "psoriasis." She said it felt as though she was "walking on razor blades" the pain was so bad. Now she could run around the stage pain free! Unfortunately, I could not get a look at her feet using my binoculars because her shoes were covering the bottom of her feet the entire time. Like the woman Dr. Nolen observed who said her varicose veins were gone (but she couldn't see her legs because she was wearing long pants and panty hose) this woman likely never took off her shoes to check that the skin disease had actually disappeared. She probably just assumed that because she had no pain she was completely cured.

DOES GOD STILL DO MIRACLES?

As each person claimed a healing on the stage that night, I noticed something very interesting: Many of the men and women "healed" claimed that they didn't need a wheelchair any more. Hinn's assistant even pointed this out to the crowd. And to prove their point, those who were healed walked, ran, or skipped across the stage to the cheers of thousands. Yet, the vast majority of those who suffer from the diseases mentioned above don't need wheelchairs for short distances. Most people with cancer, arthritis, diabetes, and heart disease don't need a wheelchair to get around in their home—or run across a stage. They might use a wheelchair for long distances in the community because they may fatigue quickly, become easily out of breath, or develop pain. If they were very sick and incredibly frail they might need wheelchairs to move across a stage, but I didn't see any such individuals on the platform.[44] These were not individuals who were near skeletons on their deathbed suffering from widespread metastatic cancer who couldn't even walk two steps because they were so weak.

I tried to imagine, as a doctor, how difficult it would be if these patients came into my office and asked me to sign a medical document saying that they were totally cured of their disease or disorder. How would I be able to tell just by looking at them? Consequently, I wondered how Benny Hinn and his staff were able to tell that these people were healed.

As I was leaving the crusade that evening, I overheard one woman ask an usher how she could retrieve a certain wheelchair off the stage. And I also wondered to myself how many others, after the excitement and adrenaline had dissipated, would also try to retrieve their wheelchairs off the platform.

It would have been mighty interesting to follow up with the individuals "healed" in the service, like Dr. Nolen did at Kuhlman's crusade. If I had gone to the lengths Dr. Nolen did, I wonder if I would have had similar results. To one person with lymphoma, Hinn said, "The cancer will never come back in the name of Jesus, the Son of God." Had Hinn taken a close look into the "miracles" performed by his hero, Kathryn Kuhlman, he would have discovered that there is actually a good chance the disease is still there—improved or not.

Unbeknownst to me that evening in August, there was actually an investigative team with hidden cameras present. Canada's premier investigative documentary television program, *The Fifth Estate,* winner of 227 awards (including an Oscar for Best Documentary), was investigating the "behind the scenes" activities. The team of investigators from the Canadian Broadcasting Corporation (CBC) attended all three of the crusade services that took place in a span of twenty-four hours at the Air Canada Centre. In their television documentary, entitled, "Do You Believe in Miracles?" their hidden-camera footage and on-screen interviews confirmed what I had heard and seen from my seat:[45]

- Hinn's ministry has delegated "screeners," whose job it is not to allow anyone who appears sick or disabled close to the stage. (The chief gatekeeper is Hinn's brother, Henry Hinn.) Only the able-bodied, healthy-appearing individuals are allowed on stage. Others are turned back.[46]

- People who are "miraculously" healed on stage suffer from diseases that are not clearly visible to those in attendance (e.g., pain in a shoulder caused by osteoarthritis).

- "At every Benny Hinn crusade there's a wheelchair section, usually located at the rear where few miracles ever seem to go."[47]

Justin Peters, a theologian and staff evangelist at the First Baptist Church in Vicksburg, Mississippi, attended Hinn's miracle crusade service at the Air Canada Centre that August. (Peters' Master's thesis examined the life and ministry of Benny Hinn.) Peters, who endures the challenges of living with cerebral palsy, went forward that evening on crutches for a miracle. But the hidden cameras captured the screeners turning him away because he suffered from a noticeably debilitating disease. Peters, who has attended several of Hinn's crusades in the past, remarked in an interview with award-winning reporter Bob McKeown,

DOES GOD STILL DO MIRACLES?

I want people to understand that people that look like I do, that have an obvious disability are never allowed up on stage. It's always somebody that has some kind of illness that cannot be readily seen. And if God is truly healing the sick through Benny Hinn, we should expect to see amputees grow new limbs. We should expect to see the severely mentally retarded restored. We should expect to see people that are crippled and have withered arms and legs be restored. But we don't. And so the evidence, the lack of evidence speaks volumes.[48]

Benny Hinn says that no miracle is broadcast on his television program unless it has been verified by a medical specialist. He says he calls the doctors before showing a miracle at one of his crusades on the airwaves for millions to see. But after the Toronto crusade aired a short time later in Hinn's programming slot, *The Fifth Estate* producers found differently. They were able to independently track down four individuals who were allegedly miraculously cured of cervical cancer, AIDS, diabetes, and a fourth unknown ailment on stage at the Air Canada Centre and televised later on Hinn's program.

- One young woman refused to talk with the producers. Remember, those who were miraculously healed in the Scriptures couldn't stop talking about what Jesus had done for them.

- "The woman declared cured of cervical cancer didn't have cancer in the first place. But something called mild dysplasia, a change in cell structure that her doctor is monitoring."

- Another woman declared miraculously cured of diabetes was found to still have the disease. "Since the crusade this woman's diabetes actually got worse—and she was hospitalized," reported the producers.

- The fourth person was supposedly cured of AIDS. But medical tests completed after the crusade showed she still had the disease.

McKeown, formerly a correspondent with *Dateline NBC*, caught up with Benny Hinn and his entourage the evening of the crusade in Hinn's hotel. Earlier, Benny Hinn had refused to do an on-camera interview with the producers. Unbeknownst to Benny, however, the whole conversation was captured by hidden camera.

Here is how it all unfolded when McKeown started questioning Hinn about the many inconsistencies in his ministry as documented on *The Fifth Estate*:

> Hinn: I'll tell you what. Why don't you invite me to come to CBC?
>
> McKeown: We'd love to.
>
> Hinn: I'd be more than happy to come. You have my word for it.
>
> McKeown: What we would like is medical proof that there was a condition, that that condition dramatically changed, and that that change continued. And we want access to the patient and to the doctor. I think anybody would agree that would be—
>
> Hinn: That's not a problem.
>
> McKeown: The basis for medical verification.
>
> Hinn: Look, I've done interviews with HBO. I've done interviews with CNN. I have no problem doing it with CBC.
>
> McKeown: I have not seen any medical evidence in any of those interviews you have given that would support the existence of even a single miracle.
>
> Hinn: Well, that's one thing I believe and one thing you don't.
>
> McKeown: But you also say you only put on television miracles, miracle healings, which have been medically verified and proven. That's all we want to do is see the basis on which you do that.

DOES GOD STILL DO MIRACLES?

When Hinn eventually discovered he was on hidden camera, he cut short the informal interview and headed back to his room with his team. But not before promising to do an on-camera interview with CBC. "I'll call you. I promise to call," said Hinn.

He never did call the producers to do a formal on-camera interview.

Probably the saddest story I ever saw was shown on *The Fifth Estate's* documentary on Hinn.[49] A young mother, Janice, had a cute little eight-year-old girl named Grace who was in a wheelchair and couldn't walk. She "was born with a debilitating variation of muscular dystrophy." The profound atrophy of her legs was clearly visible. When the producers asked Grace on camera what she wanted, Grace replied, "Just to walk."

Her mom took her to the Benny Hinn crusade in Calgary, Alberta in the summer of 2004 expecting a miracle. When it came time for people to start coming forward for their miracles, Janice picked her little daughter up in her arms and began walking toward the stage. But when Hinn's screening staff saw the condition of Grace's legs, they told them to sit back down.

Dejected, the pair eventually sat back down. Janice said, "We sat and waited, and Grace asked me if I could help her to try and walk. And that was kind of her faith in action. So I picked her up and we tried walking back and forth and that was kind of a hard moment." It was a hard moment because nothing had changed. Grace still couldn't walk.

At the end of the crusade Janice emerged with Grace still in her arms—the little girl's legs still atrophied. Tears were coming down the mother's cheeks, and Grace couldn't look into the camera. For months they had believed that tonight would be the night Grace would walk again. All they wanted was a miracle. "She cried, and she told me she was so disappointed," said Janice. They had as much faith as anyone else in the building that night. But that miracle never came. In fact, there is no credible evidence that anyone in Grace's condition ever attended a Benny Hinn crusade and was instantly and totally healed to walk again.

Will Benny be one of many who will stand before Christ one day, saying, "Lord, Lord, did [I] not prophesy in your name, and in your name drive out demons and perform many miracles" (Matt. 7:22–23)?[50] Regardless of the conclusion you may come to in your mind, I came away from Hinn's crusade that August night still looking to see my first miracle of physical healing—a healing that could not be explained by natural forces.

BROADENING THE SEARCH

Dr. Nolen isn't the only one who has scoured the globe in search of miracles and miracle workers. The *Fresno Bee*, in 1956, followed up on individuals treated by the renowned faith healer A. A. Allen over a three-week period. Not one healing of a miraculous nature could be confirmed by an independent medical professional. One particular person, after traveling nearly one thousand miles to be miraculously healed by Allen of liver cancer, died from the malignant disease a couple of weeks later.[51]

Like Hinn, Oral Roberts has openly bragged about raising the dead—but has failed to produce even one case to substantiate his assertions. Roberts' ministry never responded to a telegram from James Randi requesting evidence.[52]

Randi also requested evidence from others to support their exorbitant claims of the "miraculous"—including "miracle workers" Pat Robertson, Father Ralph DiOrio, and Peter Popoff. But Randi received nothing. Randi also requested evidence from Rose Osha, author of the popular booklet *Rise and Be Healed*, regarding her "miraculous" healing—but she also supplied no evidence.[53]

Fabricated assertions have also popped up from leaders in the Vineyard movement. Apparently, one woman instantly grew a new breast after a mastectomy;[54] a previously "totally incapacitated, paralyzed and blind" girl jumped up, her eyesight and legs restored;[55] teeth and fillings were "miraculously" turned to gold. Not only have these and many other cases (including the "gold glory dust" phenomena) been proved false, not a shred of credible, external evidence has surfaced proving the extent of their claims.[56, 57]

Controversial charismatic healer Reinhard Bonnke recently released a videotape documenting the story of a man raised from the dead in Africa. But, as evidenced by the "psychic surgeons" hoopla in the

DOES GOD STILL DO MIRACLES?

Philippines and Hinn's nonexistent resurrection videotape from Ghana, it seems that the more extravagant the claim, the farther away from North America and Europe the "healing" occurs. It's extremely difficult to verify medical credentials, interview unbiased eyewitnesses, and track down accurate and comprehensive medical reports in such remote corners of the earth. (Remember, it wasn't uncommon years ago for people, falsely pronounced dead, to be buried alive.)

Are you beginning to see a pattern here in all these "miracles"? Dr. Nolen noticed the pattern in Kuhlman's services—and I noticed the same pattern in Hinn's service. We were presented with "instant cures of cancer, bursitis, hearing loss—all ailments that no one can see." But the obviously visible organic diseases—total blindness, paralysis, withered limbs, advanced leprosy, acne scars—were never cured.[58] Why would God heal only diseases we can't readily see? And why would he supposedly give people gold crowns on their teeth, yet allow thousands of others to die of cancer and heart disease? As we see today, the sickest patients with the most noticeable organic disease never make it cured onto faith-healing stages.[59] Either the "cure" couldn't be seen or the "cure" couldn't be medically verified because credible evidence was never supplied.

What a cosmic contrast to the miracles performed by Christ two thousand years ago! Christ's healing of debilitating organic disease was *easily visible.* (And he didn't waste his time on giving people gold crowns.) In the past century, no reliable evidence that I know of has been brought forth proving that anyone rose from the dead, regained sight after being born blind, or walked again after suffering total severance of the spinal cord.

Christ and the apostles instantly cured all of these highly visible forms of organic disease and raised dead people to life;[60] we have no evidence that faith healers can do the same. Christ and the apostles healed masses of unbelievers in public; I have never seen, or heard of, any faith healer healing sick masses in a hospital or on a city street.[61] Christ and the apostles healed anyone; faith healers claim that they only heal those who have enough faith. Christ and the apostles healed completely and permanently; the number of documented cases of those who died shortly after being "cured" by faith healers is staggering. Christ and the apostles' healings were undeniable; faith healers have yet to prove the extent of their claims.

No evidence in Scripture suggests that any eyewitnesses doubted the supernatural miracles Christ and his disciples performed. The only comeback was the illogical argument that Christ's amazing healing powers came from the Devil (Luke 11:14–16).

Now, compare this to what is going on today. Faith healers such as Benny Hinn have many critics around the world who say he is not performing genuine miracles. Had Benny Hinn lived in Christ's time, Hinn would also have had critics saying the exact same things: "Benny, these aren't true miracles." Nowhere do we read in the Scriptures that Christ's critics denied that his miracles were genuine. How could the people possibly deny the spectacular and clearly visible healings that Christ and his apostles performed?

Dr. Richard Mayhue, in his book, *The Healing Promise*, describes Christ's healings as

> Undeniable, successful, spectacular, without any recovery period, permanent, overwhelming, abundant, awesome, instant, [and] authoritative, without limitations, total, and convincing all without any major medical attention that could possibly have taken credit for healing in any way.[62]

A woman once said to me, "The reason we miss so many miracles today is because we aren't looking for them." Nonsense! Did the crowds following Christ and his apostles miss the fantastic miracles they performed? How can you "miss" a friend born blind having his or her sight instantly and totally restored? How can you "miss" someone dead for three days suddenly being raised back to life? How can you "miss" a leper's worn off fingers, toes, and ears instantly reappearing in perfect condition?

If the gift of healing exists today, we should be seeing similar miracles like those recorded two thousand years ago. The fact that we aren't seeing anything that comes even close to the miracles the apostles performed is further cause for questioning the contemporary gift of healing. Clearly some things have changed since biblical history. One change was already evident later in the New Testament record, where Paul and the writer of Hebrews refer to signs and wonders as past events—even while the apostles were still alive (2 Cor. 12:12; Heb. 2:4).

I do believe, with every fiber of my heart, that our all-powerful God is still miraculously healing people today. This is why I am very surprised that faith healers like Benny Hinn have not been able to produce solid medical evidence for even one genuine miracle of physical healing. The miracles God performed through Christ and the apostles absolutely cannot be compared to what is being performed these days on the faith-healing circuit. To argue otherwise necessitates an irrational, blind faith that completely ignores the mounds of documented investigative evidence and Paul's admonition to "examine everything *carefully*" (1 Thess. 5:21 NASB).

Given the faith healers' dismal track record over the past half century in proving their claims of the "miraculous," I remain guarded toward any future testimonials from such charismatic healers as Benny Hinn and Reinhard Bonnke.

UNDER A SPELL?

"Okay," you admit, "so maybe the really big miracles aren't happening all that frequently in healing crusades. But people are still getting better, aren't they? On-the-spot healings of bursitis, painful hips, migraines, and earaches—even if temporary—are still miracles, right?"

That's the big question many are asking. What "natural forces" could possibly explain these instantaneous "cures" claimed by thousands every year—inside and outside of healing crusades? Certainly these souls are not frauds. They are not trying to trick anyone. Most are sincere, everyday folk who experience an immediate boost in strength, loss of nagging pain, improved gait, or increased mobility of a joint.

Here is a fact you might find interesting: almost every investigator who has visited these illustrious miracle services describes a hypnoticlike "spell" that is cast over the audience by the expectation of miracles, the numerous convincing testimonies, the empty wheelchairs on stage, the repetitious music playing in the background, people jumping up to claim cures, and an idolized, magnetic healer whipping the crowd up into an emotional frenzy. Dr. Nolen says, "It becomes almost more difficult not to claim a cure than it does to claim one."[63] After attending Hinn's crusade, I can see exactly what he means.

One writer ponders though, "Why would the Holy Spirit limit Himself to work in power in only emotionally charged meetings?"[64] Why doesn't the Holy Spirit work his miracle magic like this in the intensive care units of hospitals where the sickest people are located? A man with a Mennonite background raised the question to me, "Aren't these healing services supposed to be Spirit led? If so, why do they follow such a prearranged agenda?"

Indeed, why does the Holy Spirit allegedly descend upon the stadium like a "Holy Ghost hurricane" only *after* the congregation has had to sit through hours of repetitive singing, sermons on miracles, numerous testimonies of healing, and the faith healer working the crowd up to an emotional high? Why doesn't the "Holy Ghost hurricane" hit the place immediately at 7:00 p.m., rather than 10:00 p.m.? What if Hinn walked on stage to start his service, and everyone was already healed and standing at the front because the Holy Spirit decided to show up early? If it really is the Holy Spirit doing the healing, why does he seem restricted to work in only certain places, at certain times, under certain conditions? Do we see this pattern anywhere in Scripture?

Now, some might be tempted to stop here and let this "spell" created in faith-healing services explain away these healings. But you would be hard pressed to rationalize what happened in the other faith-healing services I visited—quite different from Kuhlman's and Hinn's.

HAS GOD LOST HIS ZIP?

Many individuals gifted in music, acting, screenwriting, and directing migrate to the Mecca of the entertainment industry on the West Coast of California. So it shouldn't have surprised me that the thriving churches in the Los Angeles area were blessed with many talented singers and actors. But one didn't even need to go to church to find this out.

DOES GOD STILL DO MIRACLES?

While living in West Hollywood, I attended the prominent Hollywood Bible study frequented by many of the most famous Christian celebrities in Tinseltown and featured in many leading Christian magazines.[65]

Despite the popularity of this Bible study, it was, for the most part, a quiet, nonpublicized event held in a luxury hotel. I would pull up in front of this ritzy establishment in my not-so-ritzy black Jeep Cherokee, jump out with the engine still running, and grab a ticket from the valet. And then I'd walk through the brass-trimmed glass doors and make my way across the marble lobby to join 250 to 300 Christians—most from the entertainment industry, the vast majority under forty—in an elegant conference room with virtually no standing room.

On two occasions I had the opportunity to observe an impromptu faith-healing service, each conducted by a different respected leader claiming the gift of healing—but both with a similar game plan. At the end of the evening, a leader announced that there would be a healing service afterward. Anyone who wanted to leave could (most stuck around, however). Before, during, and after the healings, there was no singing in the background. No one came out to work the audience into a frenzy. No one shouted, "Miracles are going to happen all over the place!" There was no stage. No fantastic testimonies. No empty wheelchairs. No tricks. And very little expectation drummed up in the audience. Essentially, there was no "spell."

One by one, the sick strolled or ran up to the front for healing. For such a healthy-looking crowd, I was astonished at the number of ailments present. Headaches, earaches, tinnitus (ringing in the ear), stomach pain, sore throats, stiff and painful necks, backs, wrists, carpal tunnel syndrome, heel spurs—it was a regular doctor's office!

Both healers, known well to most in attendance, healed similarly with a word and a touch. Every individual who went forward claimed healing. One young actress nervously demonstrated for everyone the improvement in her shoulder motion. Another could bend down and touch her toes without back pain. (Interestingly, those who ran up quickly to the front with ankle, knee, and hip pain, ran back cured—*at the same speed*.) Like Dr. Nolen, I didn't observe the healing of any obvious organic disease, but then again, no organic disease was visible in the room—except for the presumed paralysis of a young man sitting in the back in his customized wheelchair. He never came forward, and the healers never went to him. (I again wondered what the apostle Peter or the apostle Paul would have done in a similar situation.)

All in all, they were pretty subdued services. I imagine that hundreds of such services play out in similar fashion every week around the globe—and thousands of people are "healed." But the sixty-four-thousand-dollar question flares up: Was God responsible for these rather lackluster healings of back pain and carpal tunnel syndrome? If the answer is yes, then why isn't God routinely performing the really big powerhouse miracles he did two thousand years ago? If God's miracles of healing are so frequent today, why are so many godly men and women suffering from serious organic disease such as spina bifida, cancer, and blindness? Do they lack enough faith for the really big miracles? Is God able to miraculously cure only the more trivial ailments of our day and age?

Has God somehow lost his zip?

If these healings, however, are *not* the handiwork of God, then who—or what—is responsible?

I think you'll find the next chapter particularly interesting.

*The brain is so complex, so constantly in
motion, so megafaceted and super-connected,
that all our attempts to describe its actions
are, by nature, simplistic.*[1]

—HERBERT BENSON, MD

3

INSIGHTS FROM THE WORLD OF MEDICINE

The health benefits of faith—*any faith*—are well documented:

- A meta-analysis involving nearly 126,000 people showed that "highly religious individuals had odds of survival approximately 29 percent higher than those of less religious individuals."[2]

- If you are over the age of sixty-five and frequently attend religious services and pray (or study the Bible), Duke researchers have found that you are 40 percent less likely to have elevated diastolic blood pressures compared to those who infrequently step through the doors of a religious institution and infrequently pray.[3]

- A study in the *Mayo Clinical Proceedings* reported, "Of 212 published studies that have assessed the effects of spiritual factors on health care outcomes, 75 percent report a positive effect."[4] For example, spirituality is associated with improved quality of life and life satisfaction in patients undergoing rehabilitation for stroke, amputations, and spinal-cord injury.[5]

- Dr. Herbert Benson, in his book, *Timeless Healing: The Power and Biology of Belief*, lists a number of health problems affected positively by belief: Angina pectoris, bronchial asthma, all forms of pain, congestive heart failure, rheumatoid arthritis, diabetes mellitus, deafness, cold sores, and several more.[6]

Perhaps you already know about such faith paybacks. But did you realize such therapeutic blessings are available to absolutely anyone—regardless of what religion he or she follows? It doesn't matter if you're a Muslim, Hindu, Buddhist, or an atheist, having positive beliefs in *anything*—Brahman, Allah, Karma, even the Tooth Fairy!—can significantly affect one's health for the better. Dr. David Larson, president of the *National Institute for Healthcare Research*, says that the Eastern religious practices of yoga and meditation likely offer some of the same health benefits as faith in God.[7] Several studies back up the health benefits of yoga and meditation.[8]

Dr. Benson, also the best-selling author of *The Relaxation Response*, has studied the connections between relaxation, faith, and health for years. He concludes, "Whatever your beliefs, when you elicit the relaxation response, you'll be flexing a mind-body mechanism that has proven physiologic merit as well."[9] Sometimes just having a positive outlook on life is all you need. Another study showed that subjects who were one standard deviation or higher on the optimism-pessimism scale (i.e., more pessimistic) had a 19 percent increased risk of death over a thirty-year follow-up.[10]

Some studies, investigating the effects of spirituality on health, seem to demonstrate a greater link between healing and *existential well-being* compared to healing and *religious well-being*. As incredible as it may seem to believers, "personal spirituality" that *doesn't* include God might sometimes lead to even more favorable disease outcomes.[11] It seems therefore that any old "spirituality" will result in better health.

INSIGHTS FROM THE WORLD OF MEDICINE

This can mean only one of two things. Either God mystically extends a "health on demand" wellness plan to absolutely everyone possessing a generic "spirituality"—or our bodies are hardwired to respond positively to optimistic, relaxing beliefs—and to respond negatively to cynical, anxiety-provoking beliefs.

I believe the latter is correct.

Recent research using SPECT scanning to measure the flow of blood in the brains of "spiritual" people has seemingly "captured snapshots of the brain nearing a state of mystical transcendence"—regardless of which religion the individual ascribes to.[12] Therefore, the health benefits from a generic "spirituality" are most likely rooted in the factory parts we brought with us out of the womb. Complex mind-body mechanisms will operate, irrespective of religion.

Just how strong are these healing mechanisms? I'll show you.

Pseudocyesis, more commonly known as "false pregnancy," has been observed in women who believe they are pregnant—whether or not they desperately crave a baby. Their bodies oblige by undergoing the typical changes seen in pregnancy. The menstrual cycle ends. The breasts become engorged and sore. Morning sickness happens. Sometimes there is even abdominal protuberance. Some unsuspecting doctors in the past have been duped into thinking such women are pregnant, when in fact, the woman's body was only responding to emotional stressors via the autonomic (involuntary) nervous system. When the woman is convinced she's not pregnant, her body quickly reverts back to its normal state.

A Presbyterian minister recounts the story of a New Jersey woman who came to him one day seeking help. For thirty years the woman had required a support collar (for apparently weak neck muscles.) The minister discovered that the woman had had an abortion in her twenties, and she felt so ashamed of her action that she, subconsciously, was physically and spiritually "unable to hold her head up." After the pastor and the woman prayed together for God's forgiveness, the collar soon came off, and the minister never saw it around her neck again.[13]

Here's another fascinating example: Sudden unexpected nocturnal death syndrome (SUNDS) has been documented with disturbing frequency in young Hmong refugee men who escaped to America during the Vietnam War. Nighttime death for these men apparently came by "rare disturbances in cardiac electrical conduction," but autopsies reveal "no structural heart abnormalities."[14] Hmong refugees blamed the deaths on the culturally feared evil spirit *dab tsog* ("da cho") who comes at night to sit on their chests and smother them to death.[15] Though recent evidence suggests a possible genetic predisposition to SUNDS,[16] these "spiritual encounters" (horrific nightmares) are believed to somehow trigger the cardiac arrests.[17]

Not all is doom and gloom, though, on the mind-body front. You don't even need to consider yourself "spiritual" to reap the health benefits from bogus treatments. The placebo effect (giving a patient a sugar pill or a convincing, yet groundless, therapy) results in improvement in as many as 25 to 33 percent of patients, says Bernie Siegel, MD, in his number-one bestseller, *Love, Medicine & Miracles.*[18] Some physicians believe this figure may be even higher. When patients have high expectations, as many as 70 percent can achieve "excellent or good results from bogus treatments."[19]

One study found that giving rheumatoid arthritis patients a placebo resulted in reduced joint swelling and tenderness in approximately 40 percent of patients.[20] Sometimes 100 percent of patients get better on worthless remedies! It's thought that a placebo, through a complex mechanism, can actually release some of the body's own endorphins. Endorphin means "morphine within."

Even remote cancer cells can be influenced by our brain's high-tech circuitry. One doctor collected data on fifty-seven patients with "so-called cancer miracles"—patients who didn't die when doctors felt certain they would. Dr. Ellerbroek found that all the survivors had the same thing in common: They relinquished their resentment and overcame their depression—and their tumors shrank.[21]

One rather bizarre study gave undergraduate students plain tonic water and told them it was vodka and tonic. These students temporarily had worse memory than their counterparts who drank tonic water and were told it was just tonic water. What is even more incredible was the fact that the group who were lied to, *thinking* they were drinking vodka, actually exhibited physical signs of intoxication—even though they just drank tonic water![22] I cannot stress enough the incredible influence the mind has over the body.

"Psychosomatic illness" can be defined as bodily disorders or diseases resulting from the negative influence of the mind (guilt, fear, anxiety, pessimism, etc.). Many health professionals, such as Dr. Granger Westberg, originator of several Holistic Health Care Centers,[23] and Dr. Herbert Benson, president and founder of the Mind/Body Institute,[24] have come to the conclusion, based on several studies,[25] that as much as 50 to 75 percent—or more—of illnesses arise from disturbances in our spirit. Though I believe this number is high, it underscores the important truth that harmful emotions repeatedly wreak havoc on our health. Major depression is the leading cause of disability internationally among persons aged five years and older, according to the *World Health Organization.*

Am I implying, then, that most sickness is "all in our heads"? Am I insinuating that the earaches, tinnitus, back, neck, abdominal, and shoulder pain cured in the faith-healing services I attended were all in the heads of those healed?

Absolutely not. More than one uncompassionate doctor, after completing a barrage of tests, has told the patient, "Ahh, it's all in your head!" To ramble off such a heartless statement to those at the end of their health rope is grossly misleading and downright cruel. "The brain is so complex, so constantly in motion, so megafaceted and super-connected," says Dr. Benson, "that all our attempts to describe its actions are, by nature, simplistic. Every remarkable discovery we make only further elucidates how astonishingly powerful and elaborate is the brain and its circuitry."[26] Let me explain in the simplest terms possible, with a rather lighthearted illustration, just how the mind-body mechanism works.

Mr. Brain, Mr. Pain, and Ms. Bitterness

Although the complex biochemical pathways that link the psyche to bodily function form an extremely difficult subject to study, researchers are unraveling more mysteries every day. For example, different emotions (e.g., anger, guilt, joy, helplessness, depression) influence the release of different chemicals that diffuse throughout our bodies, such as the morphinelike beta-endorphin, the very potent stress hormone cortisol, or the catecholamines, chemical transmitters primarily involved in the "flight-or-fight" response. These chemicals affect such key physiological functions as insulin secretion, blood pressure, kidney blood flow, pain modulation, inflammatory response to tissue injury, and immunological defense mechanisms. Diseases can therefore be caused, improved, or worsened by a psychoneuroendoimmunologic path controlled, to a remarkable extent, by emotions, stress, and optimistic or pessimistic thoughts. (*Psychoneuroendoimmunologic:* memorize this short word to impress your friends at parties!)

A sort of "shut off" switch is also built into the brain. When you get up in the morning and pull on your socks, you instantly feel the pressure of the elastic around your calves. But minutes later the sensation is gone. Why? Your brain filters out these sensory transmissions as "unimportant" and blocks them from your consciousness. The brain acts similarly with pain sensations. Cortical and subcortical structures in the brain act together to mediate (make more or less pleasant) the perception of pain.[27] Evidence demonstrates that the brain, using neurotransmitters, can send messages to the spinal cord, blocking the pain signal and stopping the unpleasant sensation from ascending upward to centers of awareness.[28, 29, 30] The brain can also release certain substances that directly reach pain receptors in the periphery (i.e., hands and feet) to decrease the level of pain.[31] Several key areas of the brain are involved in activating the pain-suppression system.

Conversely, we now know there are pathways whereby the brain can send messages to the spinal cord to actually *increase* the pain.[32] Now, why would the brain want to do that? Some pain sufferers will get more money from lawsuits if they are in more pain. Some will receive more sympathy and care from their families. Some feel guilty for some misdeed and harbor the belief that if they suffer more here on earth, then they won't have to suffer as much in the afterlife.

Using a simplified analogy, here is essentially what happens the majority of the time: the pain signal calls up the brain on the neuronal telephone network and says, "We have a problem brewing down here." The brain, busy running the affairs of the body, often replies, "Thanks for your concern, but it's not important," and hangs up.

Ring! Ring! It's the pain signal again. Mr. Brain picks up the phone, "I told you to stop bothering me! You're such a pain, you know that?" and slams down the phone. This time the brain programs in the caller-ID blocking code (which activates the pain-modulating and suppression system) and the phone of agony doesn't ring anymore.[33]

Now, if the pain signal is overly persistent, and/or intensely noxious, Mr. Pain comes barging up to Mr. Brain's door. Pounding away on the "door of consciousness," Mr. Pain shouts, "We have a problem here you *need* to address!" Then the brain takes notice and tries to deal with it.

It is theorized, and supported by studies to date, that when stressful emotions "take captive" a person's mind, the brain is unable to effectively block out or soften these intrusive pain signals.[34, 35, 36, 37] When this happens, it's possible that even routine, nonpainful sensory signals from such sources as muscles and the stomach can be interpreted by the brain as unpleasant or painful.[38] The dysfunctional family of negative emotions invite itself over to Mr. Brain's place for the summer. The brain becomes so caught up in trying to deal with and kick out these unwelcome guests, that it doesn't have the ability and time to program the caller-ID blocking code—even for calls that are usually "nonpainful." As a result, the annoying phone just keeps ringing … and ringing.…

A back injury, for example, that you or I may recover from quickly may escalate into a chronic, debilitating state of pain for someone angry with his or her boss for not providing adequate workplace safety. The individual can't kick out Mr. Anger and Ms. Bitterness, and the obnoxious pain signal just keeps calling. What's worse is that even when the longstanding source of pain has cleared up, Mr. Pain sometimes forgets to "hang up the phone," resulting in the formation of an annoying chronic ringing or cycle of pain. I've observed this and similar scenarios time after time with my patients.[39] (The central nervous system actually changes on a molecular level to perpetuate the pain signal.)[40, 41]

Recent research even suggests that psychological trauma suffered earlier in life can set a person up for chronic pain. For instance, traumatic experiences such as rape, child abuse, abandonment, or the loss of a loved one might bring about structural changes in a person's brain, sensitizing it to physical pain experienced later in life. Therefore, a person who has suffered childhood abuse might feel more pain from a back injury than someone who has had a good upbringing.[42] And this pain may be much harder to get rid of. It's like giving Mr. Pain his own key to the door of consciousness. Now he doesn't even have to knock. He just opens the door and walks right in virtually unimpeded.

As an aside, I should explain that these mind-body mechanisms should not be confused with something else called "mind-body syndrome." In this unique condition, "The purpose of the pain is to distract attention from frightening, threatening emotions and prevent their conscious expression."[43] In this disorder, for example, an individual unconsciously welcomes Mr. Pain into the conscious state of mind because his overwhelming presence indirectly keeps Mr. Anger from taking over the place and exploding in a fit of rage.

Not only can states of emotional distress welcome and aggravate the pain, but it can also predispose one to serious disease and injury. For instance, research shows that a significant risk factor for coronary artery disease is emotional disturbance.[44] Back injuries can result when the brain, cluttered by emotions of anger or guilt, is hindered in properly contracting one muscle and automatically relaxing, in a timely fashion, its antagonist muscle. This split-second muscle imbalance or "misfiring" can easily lead to muscle strains. How often have you strained your back during an eruption of anger?

You see, a troubled spirit can not only *cause* symptoms, injury, and disease, but also *prevent* the body from healing itself. Harboring guilt and anxiety, in particular, is like giving your body a daily dose of a slow-acting poison. It leaches your bone marrow and gradually accumulates in every tissue until the guilt eventually kills you—spiritually *and* physically. Guilt and anxiety are extremely detrimental to one's health.

Lest you misunderstand my argument, let me make it absolutely clear that this sickness is *not in one's imagination*. The pathology—the biochemical process causing or aggravating the pain, swelling, tinnitus,

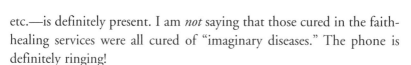

etc.—is definitely present. I am *not* saying that those cured in the faith-healing services were all cured of "imaginary diseases." The phone is definitely ringing!

In an effort to explain further, let me provide two good examples of where the brain picks up unpleasant sensations (signals) when it might *seem* like everything is imagined.

- In the average back disorder, the doctor usually cannot pinpoint the exact pathology to explain the patient's pain. But most often something—be it a strained ligament, an irritated disk, or pulled muscle—no matter how minor, is sending a noxious sensation from the back to the brain. Real pathology. Real sensations. Real pain.

- In phantom limb pain, no noxious sensation is generated in the leg or arm itself, because it has been amputated. I've treated many amputees who complained of a burning or aching sensation in their lower leg, which is no longer there. Confused, they ask, "Dr. Burke, is it all in my imagination?" "No," I answer, "the pain is very real." It's been theorized that a loss of sensory nerve input creates "excited messages" in the still intact proximal nerves, which results in "excited neurons" in the region of the brain that normally collects sensations for that particular limb. No clear-cut pathology, but again, real sensations—real pain.

Admittedly, some not-so-rare disorders exist where inner psychological conflict somehow hijacks the brain's control center. In conversion disorder (hysterical neurosis) the patient usually complains of limb paralysis, voice loss, tunnel vision, or some other physical ailment (e.g., the woman with the neck collar who had had the abortion). In somatoform pain disorder the patient complains of strange episodes of pain with no pathophysiological explanation (e.g., an elderly man whose chronic hip pain flares up whenever his wife plans an out-of-town trip).

These patients honestly feel ill—*they are not faking it.* (Think of it as the family of intrusive negative emotions all bringing their cell phones with them to Mr. Brain's place. A phone is ringing, but it's probably not Mr. Pain calling up.)[45]

In summary then, the brain, as we've learned, has the incredible power to indirectly heal offending pathology, significantly block unpleasant sensations from consciousness, activate the pain-modulation circuit, and instantly reverse "disabilities" generated from conversion and somatoform pain disorders. Under the right conditions, the brain can immediately block out, curb, or quickly cure, in a roundabout way, such ailments as ringing in the ears; migraines; abdominal cramps; pain from any joint, bursa, or organ; carpal tunnel syndrome; hearing troubles; joint stiffness; diarrhea; muscle weakness … and the list goes on and on.

What conditions are optimal for achieving this remarkable phenomenon of healing? Ironically, all the conditions already in place at most faith-healing services.

INSIDE A FAITH-HEALING SERVICE

You may never have attended a faith-healing service, but I've described several to you, and no doubt you have some idea of what goes on. Let's say we take a close look at the perfect atmosphere for these purported healings:

- *Incredible optimism:* The compelling testimonies, the illusion of "miracles," an intense desire to be healed, the miracle worker's "commanding speeches" projecting confidence and assurance[46]—all of these contribute to produce an atmosphere of expectancy, something that is very important in any healing process (including healing seen from the placebo effect.)

- *The "battlefield anesthesia" effect:* Perhaps you've heard of soldiers shot on the battlefield who didn't even know they had been hit till minutes later when the fighting subsided. Whether you are surrounded by two hundred people or twenty thousand coming forward to be healed, or even just thinking about being healed, the situation releases a rush of painkilling endorphins and adrenaline because most people are afraid of going before large audiences. Muscles become stronger. Pain disappears. Eyesight improves. And joints become more mobile. Had I questioned those healed in the subdued services I attended at the Hollywood Bible study, many would have certainly confessed to feeling almost 100 percent better before they even reached the healer at the front for his "healing" touch.

- *Power of suggestion:* Numerous studies demonstrate the power of suggestion in relieving pain.[47] Hypnosis shows some promise in treating balance difficulties, double vision, pain, and weakness (e.g., in multiple sclerosis).[48, 49] But one doesn't have to enter a hypnotic state to achieve a "miracle." Dr. Nolen observed in the faith-healing services he attended, "The power of suggestion, with or without hypnosis, can be very effective."[50] Everything done in a healing service increases the hypersuggestible state of the audience. When a famed healer shouts out, "Someone in section six is healed of migraines!" or "I rebuke your disease of ear pain!" this can literally happen—whether the healer is a man of God or a respected agnostic hypnotist.

- *Clearing the mind:* When you're mesmerized by, or just focused on, a faith-healing service, you're likely not stressed out by overdue bills, distraught over the breakup with your lover, angry with your spouse, depressed about your job loss, or feeling guilty about your sick parent. Your focus is on one thing: *healing.* When the mind clears of ruinous emotions, the body is allowed to heal.

- *Strong desire to please:* Dr. Nolen noticed that some went forward reluctantly in Kuhlman's service because they didn't want to embarrass the famous healer.[51] They may also have an either/or mentality: either I get healed or it's my fault—because I didn't have enough faith. "No one blamed Kathryn Kuhlman," wrote Dr. Nolen of the thousands who left unhealed. "Most blamed themselves."[52] Evidently, many also have a strong desire to convince themselves that they have enough faith to be healed.

Many or all of these conditions in a faith-healing service come together to provide optimal support and freedom for the mind-body mechanisms of healing. Think of these conditions as helpful friends of Mr. Brain. The muscular friends acting as bodyguards, named "Optimism," "Adrenalin," and "Desire to Please," round up and kick out all your unwelcome guests—the Negative Emotions family of anger, guilt, and bitterness—finally restoring some measure of tranquility. These bodyguards can even deal with a very demanding Mr. Pain and prevent him from banging on the door.

Even more friends come to Mr. Brain's aid, including the obliging "Endorphin" and "Power of Suggestion." They program the caller-ID blocking code and the phone stops ringing. Consequently, in faith-healing services, instant healing can occur. Don't get me wrong here: Select people *are* being totally and permanently cured of some ailments at these "miracle" services. But these "cures," as we've discovered, have rational medical explanations that don't fit the definition of a true miracle. Moreover, the usual course for most people claiming "cures," as Dr. Nolen discovered in his interviews, is for the symptoms to return again—improved or not—shortly after the service. When Mr. Brain's friends leave, often the unwelcome guests return—including Mr. Pain, knocking on the door.

We cannot deny the phenomenal power of the mind to heal. But the mind just can't do everything. The mind can't regenerate or reconnect neurons in the central nervous system to heal complete spinal-cord paralysis. It can't instantly erase the scars left behind from acne. It can't instantaneously enlarge a withered arm or leg. The mind can't create neuronal pathways in the occipital cortex to restore sight to those born blind from birth. And the mind can't bring itself back to life from the dead. That's why you never see these miracles at faith-healing crusades. I'm not saying here that God can't do such miracles. He certainly can—whenever, wherever, and however he wants. I am just saying that these miracles are so rare that perhaps this explains why no faith healer, to my knowledge, has been able to provide irrefutable evidence to prove that such miracles have occurred in his or her crusade.

Returning to our definition of a miracle, read it again carefully:

> A *miracle* is an extraordinary event wrought by God through human agency, an event that cannot be explained by natural forces.[53]

If a healing is not an extraordinary event—if natural forces can explain it—then it doesn't fit the strict definition of a miracle. I don't think most faith healers know—or care—about natural mechanisms of healing. For as Dr. Nolen discovered, "Miss Kuhlman doesn't know the difference between psychogenic and organic diseases; she doesn't know anything about hypnotism and the power of suggestion; she doesn't know anything about the autonomic nervous system. If she does know something about any or all of these things, she has certainly learned to hide her knowledge."[54]

Likewise, Benny Hinn seemed confused when he told Larry King, "Even if it's psychosomatic, it's still a miracle."[55] (Some knowledgeable faith healers, in the past, have actually been caught screening out the sick, purposely looking for individuals with psychosomatic illnesses who could be more easily cured, at least temporarily, with the power of suggestion.)[56]

"Natural forces" could easily explain every "healing" Dr. Nolen observed in Kathryn Kuhlman's services and every "healing" I observed in Benny Hinn's "miracle service" and the two "miracle" services I attended at the Hollywood Bible study. Probably the two biggest contributors to the phenomenon of "healing" we are seeing in faith-healing services today are the combination of pure adrenaline and endorphins, together with the power of suggestion: "Expect your miracle!" "I rebuke your sickness in Jesus' name!" "There's a mighty wind of healing going through this place!"

Interestingly enough, essentially the same "healing" results at Hinn's crusade could have been reproduced *before* the service even began—only on a much larger scale—by starting a smoky fire in the stadium, yelling, "Fire!" or "Bomb!" and starting a stampede toward the exits. I guarantee there would be numerous individuals who would leave their wheelchairs, crutches, canes, walkers, scooters, braces, and oxygen tanks behind and race out the exits without feeling even a twinge of pain anywhere in their bodies. Almost everyone would feel 100 percent better by the time they got outside: no pain, no headaches, no nausea, less joint stiffness, much more strength, cleared sinuses, even improved eyesight and hearing for some. But for most people, any disease process already under way in their bodies would still be present; and after the excitement had died down their symptoms would return. This is basically what happens, on a much smaller scale, on faith-healing stages every night.

Every "healing" observed in the faith-healing services mentioned above, whether temporary or permanent, had the same thing in common: All were brought about by the conducive atmosphere of wellness and the intricate mind-body therapeutic mechanisms of healing described above. A woman with multiple sclerosis steps on the faith healer's stage, running back and forth for the first time in months. A man with liver cancer living with pain and fatigue, jumps up and down before thousands of people, feeling as though he could run a marathon—twice. A young woman, wracked with pain from fibromyalgia, cries on stage because she is completely symptom free for the first time in two years.

These "healings" are not genuine miracles, but instead, evidence of God's complex design of our bodies.

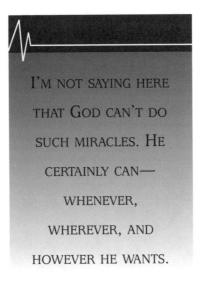

I'M NOT SAYING HERE THAT GOD CAN'T DO SUCH MIRACLES. HE CERTAINLY CAN— WHENEVER, WHEREVER, AND HOWEVER HE WANTS.

DOES GOD STILL DO MIRACLES?

*I began to look all the way back to
the Garden of Eden, at the very root of
suffering, disease, illness, injury, and death.
I saw that sickness began with sin.*

*… It made great sense that suffering
was supposed to be part of the fabric and
fiber of God's redeeming mankind.*[1]

—JONI EARECKSON TADA

4

"WHAT DO YOU THINK, DOC?"

All right," you might say, "so maybe the really big miracles resulting in instantaneous healing of visible organic disease aren't all that common in these faith-healing services. And maybe these 'faith healings' don't fit the strict definition of a miracle. But God can still heal through 'natural forces,' can't he? If it's God's will for every Christian to be healthy, can't God—with or without a faith healer—heal any and every disease through his natural laws—with or without all the adrenaline surging through a person's body at a faith-healing service?"

These seem to be the key questions of the day. But the question we need to tackle first is this: Is it really God's sovereign will that Christians always be 100 percent healthy?

Let's see what the Divine Physician has to say on the matter.

THE ELUSIVE ANOINTING

When Benny Hinn was asked on *Larry King Live* why he couldn't heal many patients in the hospitals he visited, Hinn replied, "But, you see, the gift does not work when you want it to work. The anointing must be there."[2] And yet Hinn seems to claim that he can summon the anointing whenever he wants. While I was sitting in Hinn's "miracle service," I heard him shout, "The anointing is about ready to hit this building!"[3]

Scripture, however, does not teach that the Holy Spirit, like an Easter Bunny, goes about dropping powerful "anointing eggs" here and there in twenty-thousand-seat stadiums for faith healers to find and use. In fact, the word *anointing* (Greek *chrisma*) is used as a noun only four times in the entire New Testament (NIV)—in only two verses (1 John 2:20, 27). In all cases, it is used metaphorically to affirm that all believers have the anointing of the Holy Spirit within them, "separating them to God," and "enabling believers to possess a knowledge of the truth."[4] This anointing is not some mysterious healing power—and it doesn't come and go in our world today like the friendly gas-meter man.

Read for yourself:

> As for you, the anointing you received from him remains in you, and you do not need anyone to teach you. But as his anointing teaches you about all things and as that anointing is real, not counterfeit—just as it has taught you, remain in him. (1 John 2:27)

ARE WE GUARANTEED PHYSICAL HEALING BECAUSE OF CHRIST'S SACRIFICIAL DEATH ON THE CROSS?

> But he was pierced for our transgressions, he was crushed for our iniquities; the punishment that brought us peace was upon him, and by his wounds we are healed. (Isa. 53:5)

Isaiah 53 is the passage of choice for those who claim that God provides not only spiritual healing in Christ's atoning work on the cross but also physical healing. When Christ died, they say, he died for our physical health too: "By his wounds we are healed." Therefore, all we have to do is "claim a miracle of healing" in faith and it's ours—guaranteed.

"WHAT DO YOU THINK, DOC?"

To aid us in interpreting this passage accurately, it's key that we look to Peter's interpretation of the verse in the New Testament. The tenor of Isaiah 53 has to do with redemption from sin, which is the interpretation given by the apostle Peter:

> He himself bore our *sins* in his body on the tree, so that we might die to *sins* and live for righteousness; by his wounds you have been healed. For you were like sheep going astray, but now you have returned to the Shepherd and Overseer of your souls. (1 Peter 2:24–25)

We were like sheep going astray so Christ needed to bear our sin on the cross—not our cancer, diabetes, gout, and back pain. The esteemed *Bible Knowledge Commentary* states, "['By his wounds you have been healed'] does not refer to physical healing for the verb's past tense indicates completed action, the 'healing' is an accomplished fact. The reference is to salvation."[5] We *have been healed* (past tense) from our spiritual sickness by Christ's death on the cross (the atonement).

The faith healer's mistaken interpretation of Isaiah 53:5 and 1 Peter 2:24–25 demeans the true work of Christ, which was meant to save us from the wrath of an offended God. Christ did not come to die for every ache and pain of every person in every generation that would ever live on this planet. Peter makes no mention of healing from physical sickness in his interpretation of Isaiah 53:5. From an examination of Leviticus 16 and Hebrews 10, it's also obvious that this atonement was procured first and foremost for spiritual sickness (sin)—not physical sickness.

Now, the previous verse, Isaiah 53:4, does speak of physical sickness: "Surely [Christ] took up our infirmities and carried our sorrows." Nevertheless, when Isaiah uses such words as "we" and "our" in Isaiah 53, he is speaking on behalf of the nation of Israel. For example, Isaiah writes, "When we shall see [Christ], there is no beauty that we should desire him" (53:2 KJV). This verse has no application for us today. When we, Christ's bride, finally see Christ return in glory, he will appear to be the most radiant and beautiful bridegroom ever. Just as Isaiah 53:2 doesn't apply to us today, neither does the physical healing spoken of in Isaiah 53:4. It was the physical healing of *some* Jews in Christ's day. Matthew makes it clear that this prophecy was fulfilled during Christ's healing ministry to Israel *before* his death and resurrection (Matt. 8:16–17).

By saying that we should expect complete spiritual *and* physical healing from Christ's atoning work, faith healers have painted themselves into a no-win corner of dogma. If Christ's death guarantees us a life without disease, then it must also guarantee us a life without sin. Can any healer honestly confess he or she is perfect? "Who can say, 'I have kept my heart pure; I am clean and without sin'?" writes Solomon (Prov. 20:9). "As long as sin exists," says Dr. Richard Mayhue, "the moral basis for sickness will continue."[6]

Lastly, consider this: If physical and spiritual healing are both contained and intertwined in the atonement, then dying from any disease would mean instant hell. Why? If you didn't have enough faith to claim the physical healing from Christ's death, then obviously you didn't have enough faith to claim the spiritual healing either.

This corollary doesn't sit very well with most students of the Bible who have studied such passages as Romans 8, Hebrews 11, and 1 Peter 2. It also doesn't sit very well with the grieving friends and relatives of those who die from such common disorders as heart disease, stroke, and cancer.

RELIEVED FROM THE CURSE?

In Galatians 3:13 Paul writes, "Christ redeemed us from the curse of the law." What curse is this exactly? Is it something like the "billy-goat curse" launched by William "Billy-goat" Sianis? The tavern owner was kicked out of the fourth game of the 1945 World Series at Wrigley Field because his pet billy-goat, Murphy, occupying the box seat beside him, stank too much. In retaliation, the Greek immigrant cursed the Chicago Cubs, saying they would never win a championship again. The Cubs lost the World Series that year to the Detroit Tigers and they haven't won a World Series since. Did God bring down his own "billy-goat curse" because the human race had kicked him out of their lives?

People in the faith-healing movement believe this curse spoken of in Galatians 3:13 comes from curses listed in Deuteronomy 28:21–22. God said he would curse the Israelites with "wasting disease" and "fever" if they kicked him out of their lives and disobeyed his commands. Some say that connecting the dots between the word *curse* in Galatians and Deuteronomy leads us to see that Christ also redeemed us from physical suffering. That when we invite God back into our lives, he removes his "billy-goat curse" to make us champions again.

Connecting dots is a fun childhood game—but it has no place in the accurate interpretation of Scripture. In the context of Galatians 3, Paul makes it clear this curse was our inability to live up to God's high moral standards as set forth in the Law (vv. 10–12). Paul was not referring to the curses listed in Deuteronomy 28:21–22. This is not some "billy-goat curse" directly launched against those who have kicked God out of their lives. The apostle had just finished arguing that reliance on the Mosaic Law was illogical because we are justified by faith—not works—by means of Christ's blood. If Christ bore all the "billy-goat curses" listed in Deuteronomy, then he also would have had to bear the "scorching heat," "drought," "blight," and "mildew," listed in Deuteronomy while hanging on the cross.

Clearly, this "billy-goat curse" line of reasoning used by healers is fraught with gaping holes.

ASK AND YE SHALL RECEIVE?

> And I will do whatever you ask in my name, so that the Son may bring glory to the Father. (John 14:13)

According to teachers in the Word–Faith movement, speaking forth "faith-filled" words (positive confession) and speaking in Jesus' name is some magical phrase or formula you spit out every time you want something. It doesn't matter so much what Jesus wants—but what *I want*.

Paul C. Reisser, MD, sees threads of this self-seeking health and prosperity theology interwoven into most human religions:

> If we pray, chant, incant, donate, supplicate, selfmutilate [sic] and sacrifice (goods, grain, animals, children) long

enough, hard enough and frequently enough, according to
the formula provided by the sacred text, priest, shaman, guru
or TV personality, then God, Krishna, Baal or Cosmic
Consciousness will bring us what we want.[7]

Speaking "the word," (e.g., decreeing abundance or pronouncing
health) like some magical formula in an attempt to get exactly what *you*
want has nothing to do with God and the Holy Scriptures—and everything to do with well-known cultic and pagan practices spanning
millennia of time.

Dr. MacArthur helps us out on John 14:13:

> Asking in Jesus' name means simply asking on the basis of
> His merit, His righteousness, and for whatever would honor
> and glorify Him so as to build His kingdom.[8]

"Whatever would honor and glorify Him" sometimes involves sickness (Ps. 119:71; John 9:1–3; 11:3–4; 1 Peter 4:19).

Most of us don't realize how much power is in a name. Not only does
"Jesus' name" imply power and authority, but also character: his righteousness, wisdom, holiness, love, and majesty. We need to know his
person, and be ever so mindful of his glory, before we can say we are truly
asking "in Jesus' name." Telling the divine architect what to do, or how
to build his kingdom, is utter foolishness and blasphemy.

Yet the prosperity shepherds actually chastise their sheep for praying
according to the will of God. Many faith healers say it's wrong to pray,
"God *if it be your will* please heal …" "Stop doubting and just claim God's
promises!" reprimand these teachers.[9] The late Kenneth E. Hagin Sr. (the
charismatic preacher who was known as the father of the modern faith
movement and who suffered heart disease) asserted, "It is unscriptural to
pray, 'If it is the will of God.'[10] Anyone who does so, he says, has been
"religiously brainwashed."[11]

What does Scripture say?

> This is the confidence we have in approaching God: that if
> we ask anything according to his will, he hears us. And if
> we know that he hears us—whatever we ask—we know

that we have what we asked of him. (1 John 5:14–15; see also John 15:7)

Christ said this:

> This, then, is how you should pray: "Our Father in heaven, hallowed be your name, your kingdom come, your will be done on earth as it is in heaven" (Matt. 6:9–10).
> *"Abba,* Father," he said, "everything is possible for you. Take this cup from me. Yet not what I will, but what you will." (Mark 14:36)

If Christ prayed for the Father's will to be done, shouldn't we follow in his footsteps and do the same? (See Rom. 8:27.)

"Just name it and claim it," some say, "and God will do the miraculous." That might be great—except that God never promises us that he will grant us our "three wishes"—or the miraculous. Our heavenly Father just says that he will answer our prayers *if* they are in harmony with his will. A slew of verses state this truth (Matt. 6:9–10; John 14:13–14; 15:7; 16:23–24; 1 John 5:14–15). And there is nothing in Scripture that says that it is God's will to heal every time—*guaranteed.*

SICK SAINTS

God didn't always cure his greatest saints immediately—or at all.

- Isaac was virtually blind when he died (Gen. 27:1).
- God allowed Satan to smite his "upright" servant Job with boils from head to toe (Job 2:7–9).
- Elisha the prophet, given a "double-portion anointing," suffered and died from an unknown illness (2 Kings 13:14).
- Daniel, the loyal prophet, "fainted, and was sick certain days" (Dan. 8:27 KJV).
- The apostle Paul asked God three times that his "thorn

DOES GOD STILL DO MIRACLES?

in [his] flesh" be removed.[12] But it never happened. God instead replied, "My grace is sufficient for you, for my power is made perfect in weakness" (2 Cor. 12:9). Paul also preached the gospel to the Galatians for the first time while ill (Gal. 4:13–15).

Is There a Doctor in the House?

If God has promised miracles to every believer, then you would think that God would have little need of doctors. If "positive confession" (speaking words of good health) is all that's needed for healing, as some charismatics—such as Kenneth E. Hagin Sr.—asserted, why go to a doctor? Sadly, some prominent healers have belittled believers for seeing a physician.

Since many of these souls also believe we are freed from the curses listed in Deuteronomy chapter 28, then a "positive confession" should be all that's needed to not only relieve "wasting disease," but also "scorching heat," "drought," "blight," and "mildew" (Deut. 28:21–22). You would think that with millions of dedicated believers encircling the globe that we'd all be living in a comfortable, well-irrigated, plant-healthy, mildew-absent utopia. Taking a look around, such is obviously not the case.

"Positive confession" is good for optimistic thinking—but little else. If Christ thought positive confession would heal, he would have said so—somewhere. God the Father never told the Israelites to speak forth only "positive words of healing." God, rather, stressed obedience, and designated the Levitical priests to be health officers who would quarantine the sick if needed (Lev. 13). Only God can speak whatever he wills into existence.

When your car brakes fail you don't "positively confess" new rotors, calipers, and pads—you seek out the help of a mechanic. When your house needs a new roof you don't "positively confess" the shingles, nails, and tar—you seek out a contractor. So when your body breaks down, and you're suffering from unrelenting disease, it only makes sense that you would wisely seek out the professionals most knowledgeable and skilled in treating your physical sickness.

"WHAT DO YOU THINK, DOC?"

In God's laws of wisdom, getting immunizations, having regular medical checkups, and seeking out competent medical help when suffering from sickness is not only prudent, it's expected from the wise believer. Showing up at a doctor's office is not an embarrassment to your faith; it is affirmation of your God-given wisdom.

WHO ME? I'M NOT SICK

Often you'll hear famous faith healers brag about their health status. Hank Hanegraaff, in his popular book, *Christianity in Crisis*, explored the claims made by many faith healers, including Frederick K. C. Price, Kenneth E. Hagin Sr., and Oral Roberts.

Frederick K. C. Price, now pastor of one of the largest churches in America (largest in seating capacity), once boasted, "We don't allow sickness in our home."[13] If you have faith, he says, you can throw all your medicine away.[14] Yet Price's wife, after developing cancer, underwent life-saving chemotherapy and radiation treatments. She even thanked her doctors.[15] Isn't chemotherapy medication?

Kenneth E. Hagin Sr., who boasted that he never even had a headache in sixty years,[16] suffered from episodic heart disorders—including "at least four cardiovascular crises."[17] He died in the hospital on September 19, 2003, after collapsing five days earlier in his home.[18]

The renowned faith healer Oral Roberts, who has claimed similar divine immunity from disease,[19] was "healed" of chest pains by Paul Crouch on TBN's live television ... only to suffer a heart attack hours later.[20]

Other authors have documented similar scenarios for other healers. Faith healer A. A. Allen, found dead in a hotel room littered "with pills and empty liquor bottles," died from either a heart attack or liver failure.[21] The highly regarded Kathryn Kuhlman who fought heart disease for almost twenty years, finally succumbed to heart failure in 1976.[22] John Wimber, probably the most prominent healer in the Third Wave, or Signs and Wonders Movement, wrote this in 1987 about his "damaged heart": "I wish I could write that at this time I am completely healed, that

I no longer have physical problems. But if I did, it would not be true."[23] John Wimber and his son have since died of cancer, as have faith healer E. W. Kenyon and Word–Faith publisher Buddy Harrison.[24] The renowned faith healer John G. Lake, founder of "The Healing Rooms," lost his first wife, Jennie, to an alleged stroke when he was around forty years of age.[25] And Lake himself—who claimed his ministry resulted in one hundred thousand astounding miracles of healing within five or six years—died of an apparent stroke at only sixty-five years of age.[26]

Hank Hanegraaff rightly concludes,

> Sickness and suffering are the common denominator of a fallen world.... We'll all die of our last disease. It's fatal 100 percent of the time. The death rate is one per person. Every one of you is going to make it.[27]

Nonetheless, those in the faith-healing movement often term death the "ultimate healing." (Doesn't *healing* mean to be restored to health?) If their loved ones are sick and recover, it was because God promised it. If they die, it was God's ultimate healing. The faith healers can't lose with their sham theology. Yet Paul tells us plainly that death is not our ultimate healing; it is our "last enemy" (1 Cor. 15:26).

Here again we touch on some more of the faulty faith-healing "logic." If healing is in the atonement, or if God has promised to remove all the physical consequences of sin from our bodies, why do we all age? "Look at me!" say the faith healers. "I am 100 percent healthy!" Well, go ahead—look at them. You'll notice that their hair is likely gray because the melanocytes in their hair follicles have quit producing melanin and other pigments. They have wrinkles because their elastin and collagen have started to deteriorate. And they will likely have more truncal fat tissue, and a corresponding significant loss of lean body mass (estimated to decrease at "approximately 6 percent per decade between ages 30 and 80").[28]

If you could travel inside their bodies, you'd find other even more destructive age-related processes and diseases under way in their organs, joints, and arteries: arteriosclerosis, osteoporosis, arthritis, prostate cancer, chronic bronchitis, cataracts, abnormal heart rhythms, diabetes, and numerous other pathologies (as evidenced by those famous faith healers who have already died). It's utterly impossible to separate the aging process from sickness and death. They are Siamese triplets all directly connected to our defective DNA.

If God promises to heal all our diseases, why doesn't he fix our faulty DNA that is responsible, in whole or in part, for the disease in the first place? Why doesn't he heal the destructive mechanisms of aging—the most pervasive physical sickness enslaving mankind? How can anyone truly claim to be 100 percent healthy if every cell in one's body is programmed for sickness and grinding down toward death? Someone once said, "Health is merely the slowest possible rate at which one can die."

Furthermore, a quick study of history will show that life expectancy across the globe is strongly related to sanitation and medical discoveries—not faith. For instance, across Europe in the mid-1800s, governments dramatically improved sanitation and health standards. In 284 English towns alone, in a time span of only five years, the working class death rate was slashed by more than 50 percent.[29] In the United States, life expectancy has soared from forty-seven years at the beginning of the twentieth century to about seventy-seven years today. Before penicillin became available in the late 1930s, "half of all adults over fifty contracted and died from pneumonia."[30] Did roughly twenty million people die of the bubonic plague in Europe during the fourteenth century simply because they all lacked enough faith to be cured?

If God supposedly promised more than two thousand years ago to heal *all our diseases*, why has life expectancy been so low for so many people in so many centuries? Is God handcuffed in some way by the sanitation methods and medical technology of any given age? And why did the patriarchs live such long lives *before* Christ's death and resurrection? If God promised perfect health to all his saints as a result of Christ's death on the cross, shouldn't we be living longer than Noah and Abraham?[31]

Moreover, if you take an honest look around, you'll notice that often the oldest and most godly saints are the sickest. Not because they lack faith—but because their bodies are just plain wearing out. One recent survey conducted in the southeastern United States showed that adults "over 55 have stronger spiritual faith in healing" than those younger. The study also showed that the sicker you are, generally, the more spiritual faith in healing you have.[32]

Another study examined hospitalized patients over fifty-five and found that the patients who were more seriously sick used more "religious coping activities" (e.g., religious prayer, surrender, purification, forgiveness) to help deal with their sickness.[33] Clearly, sickness and death are not more prevalent in the later half of life because of lack of devotion or insufficient faith.

In his esteemed book, *Miraculous Healing*, Henry W. Frost noted from his vast experiences that "God's power to heal, while in answer to the prayer of faith, did not depend upon a peculiar quantity of faith, or even upon a peculiar quality of faith."[34] Frost also documented in his book that Hudson Taylor, pioneer missionary to China, suffered the greatest sickness and physical weakness in his life at times when he was enjoying "his closest communion with Christ."[35]

Remember the man crippled from birth who begged Peter and John for money (Acts 3)? Peter replied, "Look at us! We don't have any money, but in the name of Jesus Christ of Nazareth, walk" (Acts 3:4, 6 paraphrased). I'm not sure the man had enough faith to even try to wiggle a toe, let alone try to stand up. Perhaps he was laughing too hard, and this was why Peter had to grab his hand and help him up. How much faith did *this* guy have? Or what about the man Christ healed of blindness who didn't even really know who Christ was. "He replied, 'Whether he is a sinner or not, I don't know. One thing I do know. I was blind but now I see!'" (John 9:25; see also vv. 35–36).

Most faith healers believe that no miracle can take place without faith. But is this idea scriptural? Gretchen Passantino, news editor of the award-winning *Christian Research Journal* and cofounder of *Answers in Action Ministries*, is correct when she says, "God's healings are perfect, complete, and absolute. They don't depend on our faith; they depend on His power."[36] Take a look at the people all around you and you will likely see very little or no connection between the amount of faith one has in God and the degree of physical suffering that person is experiencing. Take two people at random with similar healthy lifestyles, good genes, and healthy attitudes—one an atheist, and one a believer—and you will find essentially no difference in the diseases that afflict each one.

G. Subramanian, MD, PhD, and his colleagues state this in the *Journal of the American Medical Association*: The "most common human diseases culminate from long-standing interactions between many genes and environmental factors (including lifestyle)."[37] You can look at most diseases in this light: our genes load the gun; our negative emotions and environment pull the trigger.[38]

Therefore, most diseases are not the result of demons, an individual's sin, or lack of faith, but rather genetic defects, emotional disturbances, and environmental factors. (It's true that sin, by itself, can lead to negative emotions or health hazards, which in turn can lead to sickness.) We suffer mutations to our DNA, but most of our defective DNA is inherited straight from our parents. In this way, sickness and death are passed down to all of us, just as we read in Romans 5:12–21. Physical sickness is not a "spirit" as some church leaders preach. It is a disease—an inherited manifestation of the curse God pronounced in the garden of Eden (Gen. 2:17; Heb. 9:27).

This truth correlates well with the apostle Paul's diagnosis of our mortal shells: "Outwardly we are wasting away," he insists (2 Cor. 4:16), so we look forward to the day when "creation itself will be liberated from its bondage to decay and brought into the glorious freedom of the children of God" (Rom. 8:21; see also 22–24). Why would Paul say that death is passed down to all men (Rom. 5) and that "outwardly we are wasting away" if sickness is a "spirit" that comes and goes? Again, how can anyone say they are 100 percent healthy?

Consider this as well: What is the difference between dying of cancer at age forty and dying from a car accident at the same age? If God promises to cure everyone who has enough faith from sickness and disease, why doesn't he save faithful believers from fatal accidents? Does he lack the power to pull it off? Does Satan catch God off guard and cause these accidents when God isn't looking? Of course not! There is no difference in the number of fatal accidents that befall faithful believers compared to the number of fatal accidents that befall nonbelievers living similar moral lifestyles. Similarly, no valid evidence shows that

DOES GOD STILL DO MIRACLES?

faithful believers suffer fewer fatal illnesses than nonbelievers living similar moral lifestyles.

Joni Eareckson Tada, a painter and best-selling author, known throughout the Christian community for her steadfast belief in God, once believed that God unequivocally promised her physically healing from her tetraplegia (quadriplegia). She was only seventeen when she suffered a permanent spinal-cord injury in a diving accident. But after carefully examining the Scriptures, Joni changed her outlook. In an interview with Dr. Richard Mayhue, she confessed:

> I began to look all the way back to the Garden of Eden, at the very root of suffering, disease, illness, injury, and death. I saw that sickness began with sin.
>
> … It made great sense that suffering was supposed to be part of the fabric and fiber of God's redeeming mankind.[39]

WHERE'S THE PROMISE?

As you can see, God does not owe us health. You will find no passages in which God promises us healing if we just ask. You will find no passage stating that faith is always a requirement for miraculous healing. You may be surprised to learn that there are absolutely no verses in the entire New Testament that tell us to pray for healing when we're sick. (That doesn't mean, though, that we shouldn't pray for healing. Our heavenly Father does give us "good gifts" if we ask [Matt. 7:11].) The only verse that comes close is James 5:14: "Is any one of you sick? He should call the elders of the church to pray over him and anoint him with oil in the name of the Lord." Notice that he should call an elder—not a faith healer.

Yet even here, from the context of James chapter five, "sick" most likely refers to a believer who is spiritually and morally "weary"—not physically sick.[40] James is probably referring to the spiritual discouragement commonly produced by everyday trials. The Greek *astheneo* (translated "sick") "is generally used in Acts and the Epistles to refer to a weak faith or a weak conscience (cf. Acts 20:35; Rom. 6:19; 14:1; 1 Cor. 8:9–12)."[41]

In addition, the word *anoint* is from the Greek *aleipsantes*, which was used, not as a religious, ritualistic, or ceremonially anointing (Greek *chrio*), but "as a means of bestowing honor, refreshment, and grooming."[42] "Perfume and incense bring joy to the heart," pens the wisdom writer (Prov. 27:9). This anointing spoken of in James 5:14 would, in our culture, be similar to a perfume body spray or a sweet smelling moisturizing body lotion that boosts the spirits of someone feeling down. Therefore, the oil and prayer in these verses have little or nothing to do with restoring one to physical health—*but rather to emotional and spiritual health.*[43]

As well, it's interesting to note that the apostle Paul, one of the greatest healers of all time, could not heal himself or others near the end of his ministry. His healing powers seemed to "dry up." Paul didn't heal the loyal saint Epaphroditus when he was ill (Phil. 2:25–30), and he "left Trophimus sick in Miletus" (2 Tim. 4:20). Timothy, a cherished student of Paul's, suffered from frequent stomach infirmities and other ailments. Yet, did Paul tell Timothy to "claim a miracle"? No. Instead, Paul instructed him to use a "little wine" for medicinal purposes (1 Tim. 5:23; see also Luke 10:34). If sickness is a "spirit" why didn't Paul tell Timothy to give the "spirit" a boot?

As we read through the New Testament books, we see miracles of healing beginning to fizzle out near the end of Acts—becoming virtually nonexistent in the epistles. Which makes perfect sense, because we discovered earlier in this book that the "gift of healing" was a foundational gift given to the church in its earliest, formative years. The church has now been established for two millennia. As some authors have noted, one doesn't build a foundation again on the sixty-seventh floor. This temporary gift is specifically mentioned only three times in the entire New Testament—and in only one chapter (1 Cor. 12). After AD 59, no scriptural manifestations of the "gifts of healing" can be found.[44]

When my parents opened their jewelry store more than forty-two years ago in the town of Bancroft, Ontario, they wanted to have a huge grand opening that would grab people's attention. One of the things they did was supply free coffee for everyone on opening day. It didn't matter what restaurant or café one entered in Bancroft, coffee was free for everyone and the bill went to my parents.

DOES GOD STILL DO MIRACLES?

When God deemed it time to debut or "open" his plan for humanity, by moving from the Mosaic law to the era of grace, he pulled off a "grand opening" that has been unparalleled in history. Like offering free coffee everywhere to launch the beginning of a new business, the gifts of healing were intended to grab people's attention and launch the "opening" of Christ's church.

Imagine for a moment that you were a Jew living in Jesus' day, trying your best to serve God by faithfully following the Mosaic Law as God commanded. What would grab your attention more and demonstrate that God was behind this new doctrine—this "grand opening"—than seeing the spectacular foundational gifts displayed in the early church?

The book of Acts is not a prescriptive template showing us how signs and wonders spiritual gifts should be operating today. (If it is, where are the visible "tongues of fire" that should come to rest over every new convert today as in Acts 2:3?) Rather, the book of Acts is a snapshot of history, describing in detail the foundation—the "grand opening"—of Christ's church. Studying the book carefully from beginning to end, you'll notice changes taking place from chapter one to chapter twenty-eight.

Dr. John MacArthur, writes:

> The apostolic healings, miracles, signs, and wonders evident in Acts were not common, even in those days. They were exceptional events, each with a specific purpose, always associated with the ministry of the apostles, and their frequency can be seen decreasing dramatically from the beginning of Acts to the end.[45]

Again, *Christ and the apostles healed with a purpose.* God carefully planned the perfect "grand opening" for an event in history that will never be repeated. When God's "grand opening" was over—when his purpose for performing signs and wonders ended—so did the gifts of healing. Studying 2 Corinthians 12:12 and Hebrews 2:3–4, we see that the apostles' signs and wonders were already considered events of the past. Just as we would think it silly for someone to have a grand opening twenty years—or two thousand years—into the life of a business, it would be silly to expect God to re-create today what happened in the first part of Acts when a noticeable change was already evident by the end of Acts. Christ's church was built on the foundation of Christ and the apostles (Eph. 2:19–22). The church for which Christ and the apostles performed miracles some two thousand years ago is different from the church today—God isn't the one who is changing; his people are, and therefore his methods have changed … which was according to his plan all along, of course.

The foundation was laid two thousand years ago. We can only continue to go "up" from here.

What have we learned so far on our adventuresome trek into understanding the character of the Almighty?

- Though we should pray for healing when we're sick, God does not promise miracles for every saint—nor does he command us to seek hard after miracles.

- Evidence strongly contradicts the idea that "gifts of healing," such as those exhibited by the apostles, exist today.

- No evidence, from Scripture or medicine, indicates that God wills every saint to have perfect health. "Perfect health" simply doesn't exist here on earth.

- Because God does not promise us perfect health or miracles of healing, it is therefore foolish to think that we can somehow coerce God into performing miracles on demand. To do so demonstrates a self-centered, simplistic, and childish view of our heavenly Father—along with a lack of understanding of the absolute supremacy and sovereignty of almighty God. (For further exploration of Scripture on the subject of sickness and miracles, see appendix 1.)

DOES GOD STILL DO MIRACLES?

*For our light and momentary troubles
are achieving for us an eternal glory
that far outweighs them all. So we fix our
eyes not on what is seen, but on what is
unseen. For what is seen is temporary,
but what is unseen is eternal.*

—2 CORINTHIANS 4:17–18

5

"WHERE'S MY MIRACLE, LORD?"

I remember listening to a friend share a sad story not long ago. She had recently spoken with a woman whose teenage daughter was severely disabled with cerebral palsy. For several agonizing years the mother had prayed that God would work a miracle, petitioning the Sovereign Shepherd with all of her heart to heal her daughter.

But nothing happened.

Then, on separate occasions, a friend and two other Christians approached the mother. "God gave me a vision," one said, "that your daughter will soon be miraculously healed." The other said she'd had a dream that her daughter "walked upright." The mother's hopes lifted. Her spirits climbed. Her faith remained steadfast. But the days slipped into weeks … the weeks into months … and still, no miracle.

To date, this woman's daughter remains terribly crippled with cerebral palsy. I wonder whether the mother's friends realized the cruelty of their actions in showering this woman with false hope. And I wonder whether this woman's faith has remained resilient, despite the disappointing falsehood of her friend's "visions." Maybe like Job, she will continue to trust despite the false claims of well-meaning but nevertheless misguided friends.

Perhaps, like this woman, you too have prayed for a miracle from God—but the miracle floodgates have failed to release even a single drop. You read book after book heralding everywhere the existence of miracles. You turn on the TV and hear about the "miracle baby" who was miraculously revived from the frigid waters. You hear televangelists recount story after story of miracles. You sit in church and hear parishioners share incredible stories of miracles. And you wonder in your heart, *Has God forgotten about me?*

As I will demonstrate in the remainder of this book, God definitely has *not* forgotten you. Your senses might lead you to believe so, but as I illustrated in *Is God Obsolete?* of this series, our senses have a nasty habit of deceiving us. When you feel that God couldn't be any farther away, in reality, he couldn't be any closer. When you think everyone else is receiving his or her personal miracle of healing, in reality, such is not the case.

I firmly believe that God still performs miracles of healing today. But are these miracles we hear about almost every week *truly* miracles?

I'll let you decide.

THE VANISHING DISEASE

Fortunately for us, most diseases we acquire are cyclical or self-limiting. Conditions such as allergies, arthritis, lupus, and multiple sclerosis tend to fluctuate like the stock markets—down one month, up the next. Most episodes of joint pain, nausea, headaches, abdominal cramping, and skin rashes often disappear over a period of days to weeks. God has ingeniously hardwired our bodies to heal themselves.

For instance, regardless of the treatment—whether you go to an herbalist, chiropractor, medical doctor, or stand on your head for an hour every day—studies show that 80 to 90 percent of people recover from acute low back pain within approximately twelve weeks. (Though such individuals can return to work, it is not uncommon for some pain to linger or return).[1] Doctors currently debate whether uncomplicated childhood ear infections still need to be treated with antibiotics. The human body heals surprisingly well!

Though very rare, the spontaneous remission of cancer is widely documented. One veteran oncologist who had treated six thousand cancer patients reported observing twelve cases in which the potentially lethal cancer suddenly and mysteriously disappeared—permanently.[2]

Are all these spontaneous remissions of cancer miraculous acts of God? It doesn't seem so, because this phenomenon is reported most often in certain cancers, those being neuroblastomas, malignant melanomas, renal cell carcinomas, and lymphomas/leukemias.[3] If these were miracles as a result of a direct act of God, why would he choose to cure predominately certain types of cancer? When studied closely, this spontaneous remission phenomenon is seemingly unrelated to any particular religious belief or alternative medicine therapy.[4]

Therefore, we can't even be sure if spectacular cancer cures are extraordinary miracles from God.

HEARSAY

Dr. C. Everett Koop, retired surgeon general of the United States who believes in the sovereignty of God and God's power to heal, had a woman approach him following a church service. Here is how the conversation unfolded:

> "God can do anything!" [she proclaimed] … "I once knew a woman who went into the hospital to be fitted for a glass eye and while the surgeon turned his back to get an instrument, he turned back to find a new eye in the empty socket where there had been nothing before, and the woman could see!"
>
> I said, "Did you say you knew this woman?"
>
> "No. I knew someone who knows her," she conceded.

DOES GOD STILL DO MIRACLES?

"Well," I said, "could you tell me who he or she is? I would like to have a conversation with *that* person."

"Well, I don't really know that person either, but I know someone who knows *her*."

"Even so," I persisted, "I would like to meet *that* person."

"I don't really know that person, but she knows someone who knows someone...." And so it goes.[5]

In response to an article I wrote in Focus on the Family's *Physician* magazine,[6] a medical doctor, Dr. Barbara LaDine, wrote this in a letter to the editor:

> As Christian physicians, many of us probably just nod and smile politely when we hear reports of these undocumented "miracles." To question their authenticity makes others think we doubt the existence of any miracle or even the power of God himself.
>
> When my own daughter was diagnosed with retinoblastoma and required an enucleation [removal of the eye], a well-meaning person told me of someone she had heard of who had vision in his prosthetic eye![7]

Friends, if these alleged "miracles" really happened, the patient, the patient's family, and the doctor would all be on a major network TV station the next day. Why do we never read in reputable newspapers, or see on reputable news networks, eyeballs instantly appearing in previously empty eye sockets or people being able to see out of prosthetic (artificial) eyes?[8]

THE DOCTOR SAID SO

How often have you heard the phrase, "Even the doctor said it was a miracle!"? I've heard this many a time. Once, while sitting in the Hollywood Bible study, I heard one celebrity tell how she had prayed the demon out of her three-month-old daughter's left eye. When the

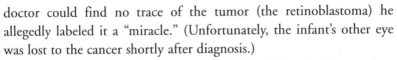

doctor could find no trace of the tumor (the retinoblastoma) he allegedly labeled it a "miracle." (Unfortunately, the infant's other eye was lost to the cancer shortly after diagnosis.)

One day I happened to turn on the TV and I heard this same doctor being interviewed about this case. "Was this a miracle?" he was candidly asked. The pediatric ophthalmologist replied, "*Maybe* it was a miracle."[9] Why was he so uncertain? Because the child had been treated with lasers and chemotherapy. The mother attributed the miracle to God, while the surgeon had good reason to believe it was the standard medical treatment that had saved the child's eye.

Another common phrase you'll hear, as in the case of the toddler with a "hole" in her aorta whom I described at the beginning of the book, is, "The doctors couldn't explain it!" Doctors can't fully explain a lot of things. Why her ductus arteriosus took its sweet time closing is a mystery. Why someone catches a cold and recovers in six days, while someone else catches the same virus from the same person and recovers in only three days is also a bit of a mystery. But that doesn't make either of these cases a miracle.

In addition, doctors, like everyone else, tend to throw around the word *miracle* at will. For example, if a patient narrowly survives a life-threatening sickness when there was only a 5 percent chance or less of living, the doctor will usually agree with the family that it's a "miracle."

The next time you hear a doctor use the term *miracle*, ask him or her if natural forces could explain the healing. The chances are great that the doctor will supply you with at least one rational theory how natural forces were responsible for the healing process.

Finally, doctors aren't always right. Some make honest mistakes and some abandon medical objectivity to treat patients with alternative therapies and drugs that have been proven not to work. When boxing champ Evander Holyfield was supposedly healed of his noncompliant left heart ventricle at a Benny Hinn crusade, Hinn—who claims to receive direct revelations from the Holy Spirit—labeled it a miracle.

Later, however, it was discovered the cardiologist had likely made a misdiagnosis because he was not informed of the 28 milligrams of morphine, 12.5 milligrams of promethezine, and 9 liters of fluid that Holyfield received in the thirty hours after the fight (which might make it *appear* as if his heart was malfunctioning).[10] In his defense, the cardiologist who warned Holyfield not to go back into the ring said he did not misdiagnose Holyfield at all. "It's basically a judgment call," he said.[11] Whether it was a true misdiagnosis or just "judgment calls" that differed over time, the fact remains that doctors are sometimes wrong in their diagnoses.

After the whole incident, Holyfield admitted, "There really wasn't anything for [Benny Hinn] to heal. That's because I don't believe I had a problem with my heart to begin with."[12]

NO PAIN—NO DISEASE?

An emergency room doctor once shared with me two stories. He was working one night in the ER and a girl came in with seizures. He asked the mother why she had stopped giving her daughter the seizure medications. The mother replied, "She has been healed of seizures, these are convulsions." The mother earnestly believed that God had miraculously healed her daughter of seizures so the medications were no longer needed.

Another case involved a woman with rectal cancer. Just after it bled the first time, God supposedly healed her of her bleeding. The next time it bled, the cancer was metastatic, having spread to other parts of her body.

Just because the symptoms disappear or seem to change does not necessarily mean that God has cured the underlying illness or disease. Just because someone can stand up out of a wheelchair in a faith-healing service and perform deep-knee bends or say he or she is pain-free does not necessarily mean the disease is gone. Numerous reports tell of people who stopped taking their medications or stopped seeing their doctors because they were pronounced healed in faith-healing services. Tragically, as seen above, the results are sometimes fatal.

"WHERE'S MY MIRACLE, LORD?"

MISLEADING MEDICAL INFORMATION

While sitting in church one morning, I listened as an elder asked for prayer for a friend who had only five years to live from a "muscle and joint disease." As he fumbled around for the correct medical term another man in the congregation spoke out, "osteoarthritis." "Yes, that's it," the elder replied, "osteoarthritis." For the millions of you suffering from the common wear-and-tear joint disease of osteoarthritis, don't panic—you're not going to die from it.

Given the vast amount of medical misinformation relayed in churches these days, leaders would do well to keep medical details of prayer requests brief and simple. The same advice would apply to most authors.

I read one account in a Christian book of a three-year-old girl, "Heidi," who suffered a broken leg along with brain and abdominal trauma in a car accident. The author wrote that the little girl "had 37 tubes in her body," and that the doctors told the parents on the fourth day "that Heidi would need to remain in intensive care for at least two months, followed by six to eight months in the hospital learning to walk again ... if she lived." Heidi, however, was discharged from the hospital eleven days after the accident, leaving the author to conclude that Heidi's survival and healing resulted from a series of divine miracles. He went on to write of other miraculous events in the weeks following the accident: "The parents laid hands on her legs each evening, and God caused the leg to grow out, healing the curve and the limp."[13]

I telephoned the author and asked him about these and other medical inconsistencies in the story. He admitted that some of the information came from the family and some from the doctors. From a doctor's perspective it was easy to see which information came from which source. Thirty-seven tubes in a three-year-old child with blunt trauma and no abdominal surgery is an absurd number. After following patients in the surgical intensive care unit as a surgery resident and on the ward as chief resident of the respected University of California Los Angeles/Veterans Affairs Medical Center Physical Medicine and

Rehabilitation program, I can also tell you that a doctor cannot—and would not—predict on the fourth day exactly how long it would take for a comatose three-year-old to be discharged from the pediatric intensive care unit and begin walking again. The doctors may possibly have warned the parents of a worse-case scenario, but the book's account never implied this. Furthermore, orthopedic surgeons are seldom worried about curvatures and leg length discrepancies in young children who have recently suffered a broken leg. Why? Because children's bones almost always grow out to correct for such deformities.

I sent Heidi's story to a good friend of mine, Dr. Andrew Samis, a surgeon who had completed his fellowship training in the surgical intensive care unit. He agreed with my analysis of the story, and pointed out a few more medical inconsistencies that appeared in the author's account.[14]

Unless you were a doctor, you probably wouldn't know these details. To you, the story would appear to be a genuine miracle. But to a medical doctor with experience treating many such "miracle" patients, this case doesn't fit our definition of a miracle. In my conversation with the author, it became readily apparent he was not trying to sensationalize the story in any way. He just didn't have the medical knowledge and correct information to fully understand the situation.

I should point out one more thing: Words and phrases used by nonmedical laypeople in books and in faith-healing services are usually so ambiguous that no competent medical doctor would rely on such information alone. "Blind" can mean total blindness, legal blindness, tunnel vision, or just plain rotten eyesight. "Paralyzed," to a layperson, can mean 50 percent loss of strength in a limb or 100 percent loss. I've heard the phrase, "Confined to a wheelchair for years," from patients who could stand only to transfer into bed—but also from patients who could walk twenty feet with a walker or walk unassisted anywhere in the home but needed the wheelchair in the community. Being able to see vague images, perform deep-knee bends, or get up and walk from a wheelchair is rarely a miracle in someone claiming to be "blind," "paralyzed," or "confined to a wheelchair for years."

"WHERE'S MY MIRACLE, LORD?"

A trained medical professional in his or her specialty, using the lab and pathology reports, the X-rays, treatment details, and knowledge of the natural course of the disease may be able to determine whether a healing is a miracle or not. Imagine, though, a layperson with very little medical knowledge, no medical training, and no medical reports trying to reach a conclusion no matter what the disease or disorder. The human body is more complex than you can imagine. Even if doctors could live for 280 years, training forty-hour weeks, they still wouldn't be specialists and subspecialists in every field of medicine. Why then do some laypersons feel they can say with absolute certainty that someone has been miraculously cured of a disease they couldn't even see *before* the healing?

TESTIMONIALS

Some people place a lot of faith in testimonials of healing. I don't. Thousands of participants every year in medical studies would testify it was the medication that made them better—when all they were taking was a placebo (a "sugar pill"). Thousands of people testify they've seen Elvis or UFOs; and some testify that they've been abducted by aliens. With tens of millions of people praying for a miracle, one would expect tens of thousands of testimonials of healings—especially given that so many diseases and symptoms disappear or improve in a matter of weeks. A layperson's subjective testimonial of healing is rarely a reliable source for determining whether a miracle has occurred.

In the early 1900s, faith healer John G. Lake (1870–1935) founded a ministry called The Healing Rooms, which boasts tens of thousands of healings. Cal Pierce resurrected Healing Room Ministries in 1999 based in Spokane, Washington. In order to be fair, I decided one evening to attend the first session of the Healing Room Ministry video seminar.

In the video Pierce read a couple of stories in an attempt to support their claims that miracles are commonplace. In one case a woman testified that God had miraculously removed a steel plate from her head.

DOES GOD STILL DO MIRACLES?

Apparently the CT scan performed afterward showed no evidence of the plate. In another example, a woman testified that she was diagnosed with the HIV virus when the doctors found approximately "35,000 units of virus" in her body.[15] Supposedly, the doctors couldn't do anything for her and sent her home to die. Miraculously she was healed.

Many believers would take for granted that these stories were true; but from a medical doctor's perspective, I had good reason to doubt. I found the details in these stories, including the alleged actions taken by the doctors, very suspicious. So taking Paul's advice to "examine everything *carefully*" I contacted Healing Room Ministries by e-mail and a registered letter in the fall of 2004 and asked permission to speak with the doctors involved in the care of these women.

I received no response.

I wasn't surprised, however. It has been my experience, and the experience of many other authors and investigators, that when an attempt is made to verify such bizarre stories, usually no evidence is provided. And when evidence is provided, the claims are often found to be untrue or exaggerated.

My question is this: If these two stories purportedly documented by the Healing Room Ministries are really true, what do they have to hide?

When you hear the word *miracle*, please keep all these points in the back of your mind. Everyone else is *not* receiving his or her personal miracle of healing. The amount of medical confusion and misinformation in books, videos, DVDs, magazines, newspapers, the Internet, in church services, and on the street these days, is staggering.

Be assured, God has definitely *not* forgotten you.

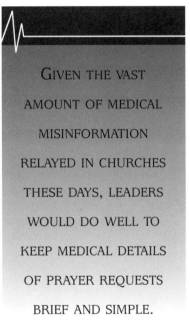

GIVEN THE VAST AMOUNT OF MEDICAL MISINFORMATION RELAYED IN CHURCHES THESE DAYS, LEADERS WOULD DO WELL TO KEEP MEDICAL DETAILS OF PRAYER REQUESTS BRIEF AND SIMPLE.

DOES GOD STILL DO MIRACLES?

Has God lost his zip? Has he done nothing significant in two thousand years? That's hardly the case. All around us we see evidence of God's marvelous work: in the transforming new birth in the lives of millions around the world who trust Christ; in daily answers to prayer; in the providential matching of people and resources to bring glory to himself; in the resilience of his church, which has survived ruthless persecution and various internal assaults through the centuries and continues to do so today.[1]

—DR. JOHN MACARTHUR

6

How Common Are Genuine Miracles of Healing?

On Good Friday, March 29, 2002, Oprah Winfrey aired on her daytime talk show a selection of miracle stories taken from the PAX TV show, *It's a Miracle*. That Friday I happened to be in the middle of writing this book series, so naturally I was quite interested. Temporarily abandoning my computer, I carefully watched each story unfold.

One story, in particular, caught my attention.[2]

Approximately two years earlier, a young mother, Edreya Espanosa, who was seven months pregnant, was rushed in labor to a nearby hospital. Upon her arrival the nurses and doctors discovered that her unborn infant had no heartbeat. An emergency delivery was carried out—but something was dreadfully wrong. The tiny newborn girl wasn't breathing, wasn't crying, and had no heartbeat.

A team of American doctors, including the pediatrician Dr. Roshanda Clemons, worked desperately to try to revive the infant. But after thirty minutes the doctors gave up when the newborn still had no pulse. Gently placing the dead infant in the mother's arms, the doctors left the room, allowing the mother one quiet last moment with her child. It had been a long time since Edreya last prayed to God, but she asked the divine Father "to please take care of" the limp infant in her arms, whom she named Iyanna, meaning "eternal bloom."

An additional thirty-five minutes passed. Still cradling little Iyanna, Edreya looked on in tears as a cleric sprinkled water on the baby's forehead.

Then something miraculous happened. The baby gasped—and started to breathe! The doctors rushed back into the room and swooped the baby up. The infant had been without a heartbeat for more than sixty-five minutes![3] The doctors couldn't believe their eyes.

The baby was quickly hooked up to a life-support machine and an electroencephalogram (EEG) was completed. The news, however, was not good. The results of the EEG showed minimal activity in the brain. "Severe brain damage," was the doctors' assessment, and Edreya was advised to allow the life support to be removed.

Edreya finally agreed. Not about to give up though, little Iyanna started to breathe on her own. In the days following she developed a suck; she could now feed on her own. On day fifteen Iyanna left the hospital, being hailed by everybody as the Miracle Baby.

At Oprah's invitation, two-year-old Iyanna, wearing a pink dress, sauntered out from backstage—a normal walking and talking toddler. Also seated in the audience was Dr. Clemons, the pediatrician who was present in the delivery room right from the start. She said this to Oprah on national television: "This has to be in the works and acts of God. I really believe there's no other explanation for it."

Although I did not have access to the medical records or directly interview the parties involved, from what I saw on this television program, this was the most convincing and best-documented case of a miracle I've come across (apart from those in the Bible). Oprah and the executive producers of the show *It's a Miracle*—Mark Cole, Gregory Ross, Robb Weller, and their respective production crews—should be commended for their diligence in "examining everything *carefully*" by interviewing the medical team and going as far as to bring Dr. Clemons onto the show.

Was this a true miracle of healing? It sounds like one to me.

HOW COMMON ARE GENUINE MIRACLES?

TANGIBLE EVIDENCE

Up to this point, we've looked at miracles from an objective medical viewpoint, explored previous investigations of "miracle" healings, and documented cases of "miracles" that weren't really miracles according to our definition of such. But one question remains: how *common* are genuine miracles like the one showcased on Oprah?

Every year approximately five million people, including "80,000 invalids," visit the well-known shrine to the Virgin Mary in Lourdes, France.[4] Many travel in desperation to the most famous healing shrine in the world seeking miracle cures. According to Kenneth L. Woodward, author of *The Book of Miracles,* the first miraculous cure at Lourdes was recognized in 1858, but since then "only 66 of 6,000 healing claims" have been "authenticated by the shrine's medical boards" established by the Roman Catholic Church.[5]

Why has the Catholic Church hired more than two hundred medical experts to sift through thousands of healing claims? Because, if an individual is miraculously healed, then that is supposed to be "divine confirmation of worthiness" for the church to declare that person "blessed" (beatified) or to elevate the individual to sainthood status (canonize).[6]

Though the Catholic Church in the past century and a half has confirmed approximately sixty-six miracles at Lourdes,[7, 8] do you know how many miracles have been accepted in the past four decades? *Only four.* Yes, out of tens of millions of people in the past forty years who have visited the shrine for healing, the Catholic Church has accepted only four healings as being genuine miracles.[9] This is further evidence that as medical technology increases, "miracles" suspiciously decrease. And even these four cases have come under some fire from medical professionals.[10]

Other miracle hot spots have not lived up to the hype. Just outside the city limits of the Iranian holy city of Qom lies the Jamkaran mosque. Widely known over the past thousand years as a pilgrimage point for Muslims, the site has attracted scores who have later claimed miracles of healing. But when mosque officials carefully examined the evidence, they could validate only "six miracles out of 270 claims."[11, 12]

DOES GOD STILL DO MIRACLES?

If God is still performing miracles everywhere on demand, as many believe, why has no TV camera captured an undeniable miracle like those performed by Christ and the apostles in biblical times? In this age of twenty-four-hour news channels, in an era when teenagers and adults all over the world have instant access to digital still or video cameras in cell phones—why has no camera captured on tape a person completely paralyzed for years suddenly being restored to full health? Why is there no footage of someone who has been completely blind from birth having eyesight restored instantly and fully?

Dr. Gary P. Posner established the Tampa Bay Skeptics group, a nonprofit educational and scientific organization devoted to the critical examination of paranormal and fringe science claims. He has kept a check for one thousand dollars in his wallet since 1989, and he publicly states that he will give the check to anyone who can prove that a faith healing was a true miracle. As far as I know, the check still remains in his wallet.[13]

Acclaimed Christian author Philip Yancey writes, "I have also asked numerous Christian physicians if they have ever witnessed an undeniable medical miracle. Most think for a minute and come up with one possibility, maybe two."[14] I have never personally witnessed a true medical miracle; nor have I met any doctor who has personally related one to me.

Though I never had the pleasure of meeting the late Dr. Paul Brand face-to-face, I personally have communicated with that world-renowned hand surgeon, leprosy specialist, and author of *Fearfully and Wonderfully Made*, *In His Image*, and *The Gift of Pain*. Philip Yancey, after spending "almost ten years following the threads of Dr. Brand's life,"[15] declared that Dr. Brand "had more intellectual and spiritual depth than anyone I had ever met."[16]

I wrote to Dr. Brand a few years before he passed away, asking him if he had ever witnessed a miracle of healing. I thought if anyone would have observed a miracle it would be Dr. Brand, who spent a good deal of time in rural India and traveling throughout much of the world. But in his letter Dr. Brand replied, "I have not experienced (or recognized, perhaps) a miracle of healing … one that requires an alteration of the laws of nature." (He was speaking here of a physical miracle, not a spiritual miracle.) Dr. Brand believed that God regularly uses the laws of nature to heal; God is certainly powerful enough to perform miracles if he desires, but the world-famous surgeon had never seen a healing that could not be explained by natural laws, ordinary forces, or by changes brought about by an alteration in one's mental, emotional, spiritual, or behavioral condition.[17]

Another prominent doctor shares Dr. Brand's beliefs. Dr. C. Everett Koop, whom Dan Rather called "the best surgeon general in history,"[18] is a committed Christian who lost his twenty-year-old son David in a tragic mountain-climbing accident. No stranger to suffering, Koop tackled the topic of miracles and healing in a chapter he authored in a book titled, *The Agony of Deceit.*

He writes,

> If miracles were commonplace, they would cease to be miracles.... It is God who does the healing, but He does not regularly do so in a miraculous way. He heals according to His own natural laws.[19]

Here is what other respected Christian leaders are saying on the topic of miracles.

Dr. James Dobson, famed Christian psychologist, author, and founder of Focus on the Family, pens this in his best-selling book, *When God Doesn't Make Sense:*

> It's not that God can't heal the blind—or any other disease or deformity. He can and He does. But to my knowledge, He never performs those miracles en masse. Let's put it this way: I have never seen any minister fulfill a promise of universal healing to all comers. Oh, there are some who would have us believe they have a magic touch. But there is reason for skepticism.[20]

Charles R. Swindoll, chancellor of the world-renowned Dallas Theological Seminary, prolific author of more than twenty-five best-selling books, and host of the internationally syndicated radio program *Insight for Living*, writes:

DOES GOD STILL DO MIRACLES?

> Not that God no longer does miracles. He does. But miracles, by their very definition, are extremely rare. In my lifetime, I probably could name three I've been aware of, and they were so obviously miracles of God that no other explanation would work.[21]

Dr. John MacArthur, celebrated author of more than 150 books, president of the Master's College and Seminary in Southern California, and broadcaster of the syndicated radio show *Grace to You* that is aired more than nine hundred times a day internationally, says this:

> Miracles are very, very rare, extremely rare, not at all to be considered as normal course events.[22]

Looking back over the mounds of evidence we've unearthed in this part of the book—from Scripture, from attending "miracle services," and from reliable independent sources—what are we to conclude? That genuine miracles of physical healing are happening all over the place? That thousands of people are being miraculously healed in faith-healing services all over the world? That God has a miracle of physical healing for everyone who calls on him?

After taking Paul's admonition to "examine everything *carefully*" we are left to conclude that true miracles of healing from God— extraordinary events that cannot be explained by natural forces—are uncommon, and extremely rare. Oprah might be able to find one or two undeniable miracles every year for her Good Friday show, but she couldn't produce hundreds.

Even if the faith healers could clearly document one or two irrefutable miracles, out of the tens of thousands they claim, it still wouldn't change our conclusion that miracles are rare. As we will see more clearly in *Why Does God Allow Suffering?* God has his reasons for not doing more miracles of healing today.

Now, don't get me wrong here: God can do *any* miracle *he* wants, whenever *he* wants, however *he* wants, in any manner *he* wants. But we cannot expect God to work miracles on demand. By saying that God *must* act in a certain way in response to our demands is to limit the freedom, sovereignty, majesty, and wisdom of our almighty God. I'm saying that God can do anything he wants for his greatest glory; faith healers are saying that if we have enough faith, God *must* heal every time no matter what. "Expect the Lord to heal you.... Expect your miracle," said Hinn at his Toronto crusade.[23] Consequently, faith healers have reduced God to the status of a mechanical stick puppet, jerking at the tug of every prayer.

Not only does this "health and wealth gospel" not fit with what we know to be true in modern-day medicine and the Bible, it doesn't fit with what we know to be true from what we observe in day-to-day life all around us. For more than fifty years now, faith healers such as Kathryn Kuhlman and Benny Hinn have been talking about a big "healing revival" that's going to sweep the world.

And the world is still waiting....

GOD'S GREATEST MIRACLE

Unfortunately, some may walk away from this last section believing that if God is only rarely performing miracles of physical healing, then he's not doing much at all. On the contrary! Just because genuine miracles of healing are rare, that doesn't mean that God is not working supernaturally all around us. *Praise the Lord, he is!* I have experienced God's supernatural power on numerous occasion in writing my books. The way God has orchestrated key events in my life to grant me the necessary resources, interviews, life experiences, knowledge, and mentors for this extensive writing project boggles my mind! Almost every day I hear from fellow believers of God's supernatural working in their lives. God is definitely at work all around us!

Take, for example, the divinely orchestrated series of events leading up to the spiritual healing and conversion of Sherri, a good friend of mine. We were in the same class together for the first eight years of school, and I always remember her as the cute blonde athletic girl who in her shyness never talked to me very much. (Of course, it didn't help that I was just as shy.) Every spring we had our annual track-and-field event at our school, where Sherri would usually clean up with the first-place ribbons. The afternoon before the meet in 1980, Sherri, who was eleven at the time, decided she was going to do some *crash training*. Despite starting at the last minute, she did manage to complete one of those two things....

Hair flying in the breeze, Sherri was pedaling as fast as her little legs would go on her oversized, adult ten-speed bike down a paved country road hill. Her collie was running beside her, panting to keep up. Suddenly the dog cut unexpectedly in front of her. The front bicycle tire hit the back end of the dog. Simultaneously, Sherri squeezed the front and rear brakes—as well as her knees and ankles together. The back tire came up, and Sherri did four or five cartwheels on her bike in full view of a car driving up from behind. In that car was a strapping middle-aged Christian man, Albert, with his wife and son.

Sherri came to rest a few feet from the culvert by the side of the road. Other than a couple of scrapes on the back of her hands and hip, she was good to go. Or so she thought. Albert brought the car to a stop beside her. "Are you all right?" he asked.

"I'm okay," Sherri replied. But when she tried to stand up, her leg buckled and she fell in pain back to the dirt. Albert jumped out of his car, scooped Sherri up into his arms, and started running toward her house, a hundred yards away. To this day Sherri can picture him huffing and puffing, his face beet red and sweating as he ran down the road, carrying her in his arms.

Reaching her home, Albert kicked their door to alert Sherri's mom. She came rushing out. "It's her knee," Albert huffed, out of breath. Sherri's mom began rolling up her daughter's pant leg. Suddenly, blood started gushing out from a large gash in her knee. Albert whisked Sherri into his car and, with her mom, they raced to the emergency department.

Several deep stitches later, Sherri was discharged from the emergency room, but competing at the track-and-field event the next day was totally out of the question.

For years Sherri wondered about the reason behind her accident. Then, in 1999, nineteen years later, she received word that Albert, the man who had carried her in his arms that spring day, was dying. Sherri sat down and wrote him a card:

HOW COMMON ARE GENUINE MIRACLES?

The kindness that you have shown to me has repeated itself over the years because every time I see a child who is hurting I am compelled to stop and help them.

Albert soon went home to be with the Lord. His daughter, Lucille, wrote to Sherri thanking her for her kind card. She also invited Sherri for lunch. Sherri, who was heavy into New Age thinking at the time, readily accepted. First, though, she had to get through her first church service that Sunday morning. (Lucille had also invited her to church, and Sherri thought it would be rude to skip church and only show up for lunch.) Sherri said to herself, "This shouldn't be too hard." But part way through the church service, she didn't feel so well. *I have to get out of here,* she thought, *or I'm going to be sick.*

With one foot already in the aisle, she was about to sneak out … but the worship leader asked the congregation to sing another song. A few minutes later, a young female soloist got up on stage and started singing a song that described Jesus reaching down to put his arms around us. *That's what I need,* Sherri thought.

Over the coming months, Lucille and Sherri became good friends. Sherri had lots of questions for Lucille concerning God. One day, while walking through the University of Montreal campus, Sherri spied some Bible tracts. One in particular displayed the verse "For all have sinned and fall short of the glory of God" (Rom. 3:23). Suddenly everything Lucille and others had said made sense. That day Sherri accepted Christ as her Savior, committing her life to God.

One day, while sitting at the kitchen table, Sherri shared with Lucille, "For years I wondered, 'Why did that bicycle accident happen to me?'" Giggling she added, "I was going to win first place in all the track-and-field events."

As if reading the answer on her mind, Lucille replied, "God knew that accident was going to happen. And God knew you would be sitting here one day asking all the questions to become a Christian."

Today, because of one man's kindness and the Lord's miracle of spiritual healing in her life, Sherri is returning the kindness by helping children at the youngest possible age. She is the executive director of a large pregnancy crisis center, providing support and hope for the pregnant mothers and their unborn infants in her city.

Now Sherri exudes the true joy of the Lord, sharing her faith with those she comes in contact with. No longer does she wonder why God allowed that bike accident, for it was her physical pain that ultimately brought about the greatest miracle in her life—the day God healed her of her spiritual sickness and adopted her into his family as his own dear daughter.

What Is God Doing Then?

There's a good chance that you agree with me that genuine miracles of healing are rare. Yet you might wonder how much nonmiraculous healing God is doing today. Could God's supernatural healing be taking place and we don't even know about it?

Interestingly, Christopher Mansfield and his colleagues, in a survey of adults in the Southeastern United States, discovered this:

> Over half of the population (58%) believes that God probably acts through religious healers to cure people.... In contrast, over three-quarters (80%) of the population said that they believe God acts through medical doctors to cure sickness.[25]

The vast majority of Americans believe that God uses doctors as his prime instrument of healing.[26]

Dr. Brand and Dr. Koop, who both believe in miracles, also believe that God almost always heals by way of established laws of nature and spiritual healing—and often through the doctor.

Dr. Brand wrote in his letter:

> In many cases existing laws of nature have been better utilized because the patient or the doctor has prayed and has been granted the wisdom to use the laws of nature in perhaps unexpected ways.[27]

HOW COMMON ARE GENUINE MIRACLES?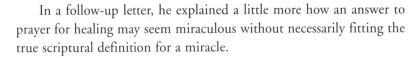

In a follow-up letter, he explained a little more how an answer to prayer for healing may seem miraculous without necessarily fitting the true scriptural definition for a miracle.

> The reality is that the Spirit of God may control the mind and the attitudes and habits of the body in a way that leads to health and healing and it is *wonderful*—not a miracle—and is often the result of prayer, and maybe the laying on of hands.[28]

"All healing is scientific," asserts Bernie S. Siegel, MD, in his best-selling book, *Love, Medicine, & Miracles*.[29] In a sense, Dr. Siegel is correct in his wording. Whether God chooses to heal by way of a rare miracle (a scientifically extraordinary event) or by way of natural law, all healing is "scientific" from the Great Physician's standpoint. Let me provide a specific example.

Pretend for a moment that you are a young, world-famous basketball player with a signature slam dunk that has broken many an NBA backboard. Your star career, however, seems in jeopardy. After suffering some fainting spells, your cardiologist has diagnosed you with hypertrophic cardiomyopathy (HCM), a serious disease that usually results in arrhythmia and/or obstruction of blood out of the heart. It is commonly considered a genetic disorder and is the leading cause of sudden cardiac death in adolescent and preadolescent children. You've been very fortunate up to this point in your life that you haven't dropped dead on the basketball court.

"The medications are not working well enough," says the cardiac surgeon; "you need a special procedure."

"What kind of procedure?" you ask.

"A catheter septal ablation."

"A catheter steeple what—?"

"Using a long thin tube, we inject 96 percent ethanol down the first septal branch of the left descending artery of your heart, essentially causing a heart attack."

"A heart attack! No Dr. Jekyll is going to give me a heart attack on the operating table! I'd sooner die on the court!"

"You will if you keep playing against my advice. It's a procedure that's been used with great success since the early 1990s. It causes a therapeutic heart attack that kills off some of the heart tissue in the septum, allowing for better blood flow out of your heart."

But you protest, "My reflexologist swears that with just eighty-nine more weeks of treatments my heart disease will disappear."

"In eighty-nine more weeks you'll probably be playing a game of twenty-one with God," says the cardiac surgeon. "And you'll lose. Take it or leave it."

All this news hits you like a transport truck carrying nitroglycerin. "What are the chances I'll still be alive in five years without the procedure?"

"In your serious situation, probably twenty percent."

"And if I do have the operation?"

"Chances are greater than ninety percent you'll still be alive."

After pondering it, you agree to have a heart attack. Try explaining this one to Mom.

A hundred years ago, with your serious HCM, a physical miracle probably would have been needed to keep you alive past the age of fifty. (But considering how rare miracles are, chances are, God would have allowed you to die.) Today, however, because of advances in medicine, evidence of God's mercy on our generations, your chances of pulling through the procedure and surviving for at least five years are greater than 90 percent (hypothetically speaking).

What good will prayer do?

Suppose that, unknown to you and the surgeons, you are in the 10 percent group who will die even with the surgery. It might take a divine miracle to save you—or maybe God can accomplish it by using the laws of nature. What can God do? The Great Physician can give the surgeons wisdom and the stability of mind and hand to expertly carry out the procedure, along with the clarity of intellect to choose the best post-procedure medications and treatment options.

God can also, through an almost miraculous series of events, allow the critical-care nurses to discover a serious complication that would otherwise have gone undetected until it was too late. God can pre-arrange a particular intensive care room that doesn't have a potentially deadly bacteria lurking inside. Or God can maximize the serum levels of a drug, or maximize the body's immune system to fight off deadly organisms. God could do literally hundreds of things to take you out of the hypothetical 10 percent "death" group and move you into the 90 percent "survival" group. And none of these interventions would really fit our definition of a miracle.

Because we don't know which group you were destined for, it's impossible to prove on an individual basis whether God's divine intervention was at play. Did the series of events all work out in your favor by "chance"? Or did God have something to do with it? Unlike irrefutable miracles, we have no way to prove how God uses the natural laws of healing to direct the outcome. A physical miracle is usually obvious—not so when God decides to heal using his established laws.

> SHOULD WE PRAY FOR HEALING? ABSOLUTELY! PRAY WITH ALL THE FAITH YOU CAN MUSTER THAT IF IT IS GOD'S WILL TO PERFORM A MIRACLE, HEAL QUICKER, OR DELAY DEATH—HE WILL!

Nevertheless, this we can say with absolute certainty: *God does not offer healing to every person who asks for it.* How do we know? Because everyone eventually gets sick, and everyone eventually dies. The godliest saints fall prey to sickness such as heart disease, stroke, and cancer, and die like everyone else—some at a very young age. For whatever reason, God does not directly intervene in the health crisis of every saint. (We will explore the reasons in another book, when we tackle the tough questions, "Why does God allow his saints to suffer? And why isn't God performing more miracles?")

If we look back in history, we notice something very interesting.

DOES GOD STILL DO MIRACLES?

Two thousand years ago Christ did many miracles of *physical healing,* but his disciples must have wondered why there were not more miracles of *spiritual healing.* Where were the tens of thousands of miracles of genuine conversions? Scores of people were following Christ, but the vast majority were only interested in seeing the spectacular miracles Jesus performed. For the most part, they were a wicked generation who crucified Christ (Matt. 16:4; Mark 8:11–12).

Today things are nearly the opposite. Miracles of *spiritual healing* can be found almost everywhere we turn; but even when we search for it, we have extreme difficulty coming up with even one miracle of *physical healing* (further evidence that God often works differently in different ages.) All around us we see the miraculous transformation of lives, possible only through the Holy Spirit's drawing and his effectual work in a person's life, taking someone who is "dead in your trespasses and sins" and raising him or her to spiritual life! (Eph. 2:1–5 NASB; John 6:44). Even Benny Hinn admits in his crusades, "The greatest miracle is not a physical healing. The greatest miracle is not even the raising of the dead. The greatest miracle is salvation."[30] The salvation of a soul is the greatest miracle of all—greater and more meaningful than all the miracles of physical healing put together (John 5:20–21).

If you have become discouraged because God is not working a personal miracle of healing in your life, I would encourage you to meditate on the miracles that God is doing all around you. The spiritual transformation of a soul from death to life is truly the greatest miracle of all. Only by understanding this can you fully appreciate God's personal and intimate working in your own life.

The last thing I want to do is discourage any of you from praying for healing. Should we pray for healing? *Absolutely!* Pray with all the faith you can muster that if it is God's will to perform a miracle, heal quicker, or delay death—he will! Do you want healing from cancer? Pray for it! Do you want healing from your diabetes? Pray for it! Do you want the inexpressible peace and comfort that only the Holy Spirit can provide? Pray for it!

A month or so after sending a thank-you letter to Dr. Brand, I received, unexpectedly, a second letter from the famous surgeon. In it he strongly encouraged me to emphasize the power of prayer in my book. He wrote,

> I have no doubts whatever that as we pray the Holy Spirit does help the sick individual to experience positive changes in his outlook and to face his sickness—or even his death—in a way that is healthy and that helps him to utilize physical resources and mental and emotional resources which are profoundly useful in developing health and either in postponing death or making it into a positive experience.[31]

Dr. Gordon D. Fee is an ordained minister of the Assemblies of God. I love his response to the question, "Why pray?"

> No healing has ever been deserved; it is always an expression of God's grace…. The mystery of faith is that there is a wonderful correlation between our asking and trusting, and what goes on about us. God doesn't have to answer prayer, but He does. God doesn't have to heal, but He graciously does. Healing, therefore is not a divine obligation; it is a divine gift. And precisely because it is a gift, we can make no demands. But we can *trust* Him to do all things well![32]

If you are sick, I would encourage you to pray for healing. But I would also encourage you to rest contentedly in God's grace, goodness, and perfect sovereign will, confidently trusting him to do what is best.

SOLOMON'S CLUE #7

Chasing explosions,
have you lost your way?
Grab hold of your lamp,
trade the black for day.

7

SOLOMON'S CLUES

Perhaps you think I went a bit overboard on the subject of miracles in the previous chapters. Maybe you're wondering why I've dedicated so many pages to trying to convince you that true miracles of healing are very rare. Perhaps you're curious as to why I've emphasized so emphatically the true definition of a miracle—or why I've painstakingly detailed so many medical insights in an attempt to help you better understand the complexities of the human body. What does all this have to do with understanding the character of God?

As you'll see in the next book, *it has everything to do with understanding the Divine.* It's *impossible* for us to properly arrange our stepping-stones on the issue of suffering without first grasping the truths of miracles—especially miracles of healing. When a caller on the *Larry King Live* show asked televangelist Kenneth Copeland why God doesn't always heal, Copeland replied that the fault lies at the receiving end rather than the giving end. "If we are not receiving [healing]," said Copeland, then "there is a misconnection, a breakdown, there in spiritual communication."[1] Benny Hinn tells us how people can be healed at his crusades, only to become sick again: "The reason people lose their healing is because they begin questioning whether God really did it."[2] In other words, according to Kenneth Copeland and Benny Hinn, sickness is *always* our fault!

This is what my grandmother, at the age of seventy-two, also believed as I watched her battle the horrifying illness of breast cancer. She had donated hundreds of dollars to Copeland's and Hinn's ministries. She also had so much faith in God that one day she confided to my mother, "When I finally beat this cancer I'm going to write an article to *Reader's Digest* and tell everyone what my Jesus did for me!"

She never got a chance to write that article. My grandmother had more faith in God's power to heal than anyone I know—yet she still succumbed to the cancer. Even though she didn't say very much at the time, I knew that her belief in "God's absolute promise to heal" was tearing her apart on the inside as her physical body wasted away on the outside. If you believe, like Copeland, that most or all sickness and suffering is caused from a "breakdown in spiritual communication" on the receiver's part, then you will *never* understand God on the issue of suffering. And you will likely find yourself, at some point in life, deeply depressed, bitter, and distraught as you personally come face-to-face with relentless suffering and death.

A woman, blind from birth, wrote a heartrending letter to Hank Hanegraaff, the president and chair of the Christian Research Institute, who has received hundreds of such letters from distraught Christians over the years. In it she told of how her church had denounced her for her lack of faith and disobedience—the only reasons why God would not cure her blindness.

She wrote,

> I spent hours, sleepless nights, agonizing over the issue. I became depressed and began to lose my joy. I even quit praying. Some Sundays I simply couldn't stand church because I felt like an outsider in God's family, watching His pet children get "blessed" because of their "Faith."… If I was doing or not doing something that hindered God, I was at a loss trying to discern what it was.[3]

Similar scenarios sadly play out hundreds of times every week across America. The words coming out of the mouths of some church leaders and faith healers are downright cruel. Benny Hinn insinuated on his television program that if you had enough faith, you could lay your dead loved one in front of the TV and she or he would be raised back to life. Hinn said, "I want to take my dead loved one and place them in front of that TV set for twenty-four hours. Placing them before a television set waiting for God's power to come through and touch them."[4] There is no evidence whatsoever that anyone has been raised back from the dead after being placed in front of the TV broadcasting Hinn's program. If someone isn't raised back to life, then was it a lack of faith on the relative's part? Giving people false hope like this is like driving another dagger into their already-wounded spirits. As one family member of a coal miner killed in the tragic 2006 West Virginia mine accident said, "The only thing worse than no hope, is to be given false hope."[5]

Cal Pierce, the director of the Healing Rooms Ministries, has this printed on his Web site: "God is not raising up an army to go to battle on crutches."[6] (Pierce, of course, is referring here to those who are physically disabled.) I wonder how the woman mentioned above, blind from birth, would feel after hearing yet another demoralizing statement like this from a fellow Christian? I wonder how believers, paralyzed from the neck down like Joni Eareckson Tada, would feel after hearing that they just don't make the cut in God's army because they can't walk? Again, another dagger gets thrust into a believer's already-wounded spirit.

Fortunately, Joni knows better, and she understands that she is vigilantly fighting on the front lines of God's elite army. But many other disabled believers don't understand this.

The deleterious emotions suffered by already-wounded saints can easily lead to downward spiraling effects on their health. When someone who is desperate for a miracle is told to expect a miracle of physical healing, and then that genuine miracle never comes (which is almost always the case), the individual may very likely get sicker. One study showed that hospitalized patients over fifty-five who "felt punished by God for their lack of devotion," "wondered whether God had abandoned them," "voiced anger that God didn't answer their prayers," or thought the Devil was behind their illnesses, were found to have statistically significant "poorer physical health, worse quality of life, and greater depression."[7, 8]

Dr. Kenneth I. Pargament and his colleagues went a step further in their landmark study. They discovered that patients over fifty-five who "felt alienated from or unloved by God and attributed their illness to the Devil were associated with a 19% to 28% increase in risk of dying during the approximately 2-year follow-up period."[9]

But the authors didn't stop here. In their follow-up study published three years later, they looked very closely at the 268 survivors. And they found that there was a significant connection between poorer quality of life and the survivors' belief that God was punishing them, thinking the Devil was behind their illness, or doubting God's powers. Declines in physical function were linked to patients who were pleading with God for a miracle, and those who thought the Devil was behind their illness. And declines in physical and mental health were tied to the belief that God was punishing them.[10]

Overall, the authors found that negative religious coping strategies arising from certain spiritual beliefs and attitudes are linked to poorer health, poorer quality of life, decreased function, and increased mortality in those over fifty-five years of age who are ill.

Why have I stressed so earnestly the definition of a miracle? Why did I trek off to "miracle services" to personally document what is going on? Why have I defended my arguments with so many Scripture verses and investigative studies? Folks, we are virtually *killing* our brothers and sisters by promoting the illusion that miracles are commonplace. We are ripping to shreds the souls of the sickest saints by telling them to expect a miracle. Yes, thousands of people in healing crusades are getting better—almost all of them by proven mind-body mechanisms of physical and spiritual healing. But as Dr. Nolen, I, and several others have documented, thousands of the most critically ill and disabled individuals are leaving these crusades without a miracle. In addition, millions more critically ill individuals watching these faith healers on television are not being healed. The negative emotions that ensue, including devastating guilt, bitterness, and hopelessness, are making these souls sicker. Faith healers, overall, with their illusions of miracles and their "expect a miracle" doctrine, may actually be responsible for *more* sickness and death in this world than what they claim to be healing—or preventing.

Perhaps you disagree, though. You might respond as a friend of mine once did: "Why do you find it necessary to explain miracles? Why not just give God the benefit of the doubt and call it a miracle?" Like many, he was upset that I would even think about questioning a miracle from a medical perspective.

I pointed out to my friend that the spectacular healings performed by Christ and the apostles had no medical explanation whatsoever. But this did little to appease his indignation. Why is it so important that we stick to our definition so closely and label as miracles only healings that cannot be explained by natural forces? Why not just call every astonishing healing a miracle?

> MANY CHRISTIANS IN MODERN EVANGELICALISM HAVE BUILT THEIR ENTIRE "GOD MOSAIC" ON SHIFTING SUBJECTIVE EXPERIENCES—ON FEELINGS, EMOTIONS, HUNCHES, VISIONS, PROPHECIES, TESTIMONIALS, EXPERIENCES, AND "MIRACLES."

The reason is simple: Calling some healings "miracles" if they can be partially or fully explained by modern medicine demeans the spectacular miracles performed by Christ and the apostles. Their miracles were without medical explanation. The healings they performed were true miracles!

As evidenced above, it is also a matter of life and death. We are discouraging millions of Christians to the point of physical death by

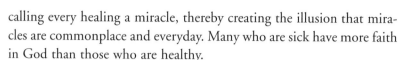

calling every healing a miracle, thereby creating the illusion that miracles are commonplace and everyday. Many who are sick have more faith in God than those who are healthy.

For these reasons, I believe it would be best for Christ's body of believers if the term *miracle* were reserved for an extraordinary event—something that cannot be explained by natural forces.

As mentioned earlier in the book, the topic of miracles is definitely a very sensitive and challenging topic to explore. Is there any wisdom that we can draw on to help get us past this difficult hurdle on our journey?

In *Is God Obsolete?* we were given some fictional clues by Solomon just after we won ten million dollars in a rather bizarre game show. These clues, based on biblical principles, are provided to help us avoid some nasty pitfalls and obstacles on our quest into understanding God more. Clue number seven, given below, is quite timely as we near the end of this book on miracles of healing.

Chasing explosions, have you lost your way?

Grab hold of your lamp, trade the black for day.

What Exactly Is Solomon Getting at Here?

False expectations of God can be insurmountable obstacles on our journey into understanding the Divine. Dr. James Dobson says these expectations "set us up for disillusionment. There is no greater distress in human experience than to build one's entire way of life on a certain theological understanding, and then have it collapse at a time of unusual stress and pain."[11]

Many Christians in modern evangelicalism have built their entire "God mosaic" on shifting subjective experiences—on feelings, emotions, hunches, visions, prophecies, testimonials, experiences, and "miracles." I had a friend tell me of his encounter with a father who based all his beliefs about God's existence and character on one incident in which God "miraculously" healed his son. "A simple man believes anything," writes Solomon, "but a prudent man gives thought to his steps" (Prov. 14:15).

Miracle addicts, as a group, don't give much thought to their steps. And they usually don't want to hear the real truth behind many fabricated or exaggerated stories of "miracles." Instead, many wander through life gazing up into the sky, waiting for the next miracle fix to appease their craving for the supernatural—waiting for God to light their path with his divine fireworks. The miracle seeker's journey becomes one of erratic sprints and stops in the darkness, sustained by hope that the next miracle explosion will illuminate the way—often leading to discouragement when it doesn't.

Consequently, such souls tragically fall victim to nearly every conceivable hazard in their journey into understanding God. Because their understanding is grounded primarily in the quicksand of esoteric experiences, instead of the bedrock of God's holy Word, they often fall prey to miracle-touting leaders who sell the illusion of miracles like crack cocaine—hooking their victims into a life filled with disillusionment, frustration, emptiness, and despair. The illusion of physical miracles often distracts these miracle addicts away from the one true God, sending them instead down dark and forbidden paths teeming with all manner of error and spiritual sickness.

Admittedly, there are many dedicated Christians who attend faith-healing services who also diligently study God's Word and witness to their friends. David, the man I sat beside at a Benny Hinn crusade, was such a person.[12] This guy was so on fire for God that I expected him to spontaneously combust at any second! After the crusade, I spoke with David on the phone. He talked for several minutes, and during that time I don't think he let a sentence go by in which he wasn't praising God for something or other, or extolling God's power, or telling me how God was supernaturally working through his life. He was quoting Scripture verses from all over the Bible, seemingly having a verse for everything he believed.

The more he talked, the more apparent it became that David was passionate about seeking out God's truth. Unfortunately, he had fallen under the preaching of some who had led him astray. He desperately wanted the truth, but these powerfully deceptive experiences of "miracles," "visions," and "prophecies" had blinded him from objectively seeing God's Word. He was also blinded from seeing all the sickness and suffering even in churches that believe God promises to heal us if we have enough faith. I felt a strong compassion for David. And I wondered how many dedicated Christians there are out there just like him, who have been led astray from the truth by their senses and by false teachers. No doubt, out of more than twenty thousand people at the Benny Hinn miracle service that night, David was the person God had planned for me to meet.

Unlike David, however, there are many who seek hard proof of the supernatural while overlooking one of the greatest miracles staring them in the face: *God's Word.* If most miracle seekers truly understood the miraculous treasure they held in their hands, they would never crave another miracle fix. They would never find themselves distraught, frustrated, and lost, stumbling around in the darkness. Nor would they lack the "inexpressible and glorious joy" that is characteristic of a godly believer (1 Peter 1:8).

Instead of chasing after "miracle explosions" for direction, the psalmist chose the best means of guidance: "Your word is a lamp to my feet and a light for my path" (Ps. 119:105).

> We live by faith, not by sight. (2 Cor. 5:7)
> But examine everything *carefully*; hold fast to that which is good. (1 Thess. 5:21 NASB)

When someone is healed, should we give God the "benefit of the doubt"?

Absolutely! Give God all the praise and glory rightfully due his blessed name for *every* healing—no matter what the exact mechanism of the healing may be. We can believe that God is healing people today of their diseases and disorders, while at the same time believing that supernatural miracles of physical healing are indeed rare.

Why is it so important on our journey into understanding God to take this truth to heart? Because the only way to understand God on the complex issue of suffering in *Why Does God Allow Suffering?* is to understand God's justice from Genesis through Revelation. And it is impossible to gain a decent understanding of the justice and wisdom of

God if one is blinded by the belief that miracles of physical healing are promised, commonplace, and for the asking. There will come a day, I guarantee you, when you or someone close to you will fall ill and die. And like my grandmother, who battled the horridness of breast cancer in her last dying months, if you do not have a strong grasp of God's justice you will have little or no understanding of why God would allow you or your loved one to endure these trials.

Despite the fact that miracles of physical healing are rare, I still encourage you to pray, pray, pray! Unexpected healings are always wonderful, whether they can be explained by natural forces or only by a miracle from the hand of God. But I encourage everyone to reserve the term *miracle* for healings that fit the precedent set by Christ and the apostles. By doing so, I believe it will give us a head start on our journey into understanding the character of almighty God on issues of suffering. It will also foster to the greatest degree possible the spiritual and physical health of the body of Christ.

SCENES FROM THE JOURNEY AHEAD

Perhaps this book has really helped you to understand what is going on in our miracle-obsessed world. But maybe these chapters have left you with one unanswered question: *Why isn't God performing more miracles of physical healing?*

This is the question of the day. It's also a question that few books (if any) have directly addressed. But no question should be off-limits in our never-ending journey into understanding God more.

Here's a quick look at the other books in An MD Examines:

IS GOD OBSOLETE?

Nearly everyone at some point in life questions God's ability to run the universe. But are we asking the proper questions, from the proper perspective, based on a proper understanding of the Almighty? What might we have in common with a four-year-old? You might be surprised to discover the similarities as we explore the "personal spirituality" craze overtaking the

DOES GOD STILL DO MIRACLES?

world. Has God become, in a sense, obsolete? This first book in the series is packed with gripping anecdotes and lively illustrations—from trying to resuscitate a gangbanger's exposed heart to participating in one of the most bizarre futuristic game shows ever concocted. This minibook is a great resource to pass along to believers and nonbelievers alike—and the perfect beginning to the series An MD Examines.

WHY DOESN'T GOD STOP EVIL?

How often do we look with dismay at the mess in our world and ask, "What was God thinking?" If there really is a good God up above, why is there so much evil in this world? If God is all-powerful, why didn't he bind up or destroy the Devil right from the beginning? If heaven is so great, why didn't God send us straight to paradise and forget earth all together? Where was God on September 11? And where was God when Hurricane Katrina struck? These and many other difficult questions are tackled head-on, providing fresh insight into some of the toughest questions ever asked of the Almighty. When the subject of evil is closely examined, we discover that there is a strong vein of wisdom and compassion in God's justice that Christendom has failed to recognize.

WHY DOES GOD ALLOW SUFFERING?

In this book we'll use the insight and understanding gained from the other books in the series to help us answer one of the toughest questions ever asked of the Almighty: How can a God of love allow his children to suffer? Several inspiring true stories are presented, including the stirring account of how Steven Curtis Chapman faced the "thunder and lightning" in his life. This book goes further than most books on suffering by using illustrations and analogies to help the reader better understand the root cause of why we suffer. It also contains a unique story that helps us understand the real question at the heart of the matter: How can God be altogether just, kind, holy, righteous, and loving in the midst of our suffering? (See Jer. 9:24.)

At the end of each book we'll continue to examine a part of Solomon's fictional clues for some vital and practical insight into our Creator. By doing so, we'll break past the conflict barrier to illustrate the five levels of intimacy with our heavenly Father. And as always, we won't give up no matter how treacherous the waters, how yawning the valleys, or how lofty the mountains. An understanding of God will radically affect our lives like nothing else!

READERS' GUIDE
FOR PERSONAL REFLECTION OR GROUP DISCUSSION

CHAPTER 1
THE GREATEST MIRACLE WORKER

1. According to the author, why were miracles—also called signs and wonders—performed during certain periods of time recorded in the Bible?

2. What six characteristics did Christ's miracles of healing display? Can you think of any other elements that characterize Christ's miracles of healing?

3. The author believes that miracles of healing were not intended to bring great numbers of people to faith in God. What Bible passage does he quote to substantiate his position? If not meant to bring people to faith, what is the purpose of miracles of healing?

CHAPTER 2
FAITH HEALERS: GOD'S SERVANTS
OR GOD'S EMBARRASSMENTS?

1. What has your opinion been of the faith healers discussed in the first part of the chapter? Does the possibility of fraud in the cases mentioned prove that all faith healings since the time of Christ and the apostles are frauds? Why or why not?

2. Dr. Kenneth A. Nolen did an exhaustive investigation of miraculous cures claimed by faith healer Kathryn Kuhlman. What were his findings?

3. The author himself witnessed firsthand a Benny Hinn healing crusade. What were his impressions? Do you think it likely or unlikely that physical healings occurred at this crusade? Why or why not?

4. What is the common element among those who are claimed to have been cured at healing ministries like those of Kathryn Kuhlman and Benny Hinn? How does this compare to healings Jesus did?

CHAPTER 3
INSIGHTS FROM THE WORLD OF MEDICINE

1. Research has shown that a positive outlook on life results in greater physical well-being. How can faith help build up that positive outlook?

2. It appears that mere spirituality, as opposed to a specific belief in God, produces increased physical well-being. What accounts for this, according to the author? A related phenomenon is the "placebo effect." What is this, and how does it work?

3. How do some of the mind-body mechanisms of healing in various diseases described in this chapter relate to faith-healing services? Some of these processes apparently result in actual cures in these faith-healing services. Does that make these healings miraculous or merely the result of natural processes? What bearing does the author's definition of a miracle have on your answer to the previous question?

4. What did every healing that occurred in the services described in this chapter have in common? If these healings are not genuine miracles, what are they?

CHAPTER 4
"WHAT DO YOU THINK, DOC?"

1. What is the scriptural definition of *anointing*, and how many times is it used in the Bible? Is the biblical understanding of the term the same as Benny Hinn's? If not, how do they differ?

2. Some claim scriptural support for the idea that Christ came to die—and provide healing—for our physical wounds and diseases. Is this an accurate interpretation of the relevant Bible passages? Why or why not? What can we say, in general, about faith

DOES GOD STILL DO MIRACLES?

healers' interpretation of various Old and New Testament passages that seem to relate faith healing to Christ's atoning work?

3. What is "positive confession"? Do you think it works? What do you think of the author's comparison of positive confession in relation to bodily malfunctions with positive confession in relation to automotive breakdowns or house repairs?

4. What were your thoughts in response to the examples of Kenneth K. C. Price, Kenneth E. Hagin Sr., and Oral Roberts in relation to their claims about faith healings for themselves? How do those in the faith-healing movement get around these apparent contradictions?

5. Did the healings recorded in the Bible depend on a strong faith on the part of the one receiving healing? Give scriptural support for your answer.

CHAPTER 5
"WHERE'S MY MIRACLE, LORD?"

1. What was the conclusion to the widely proclaimed healing incident of famous boxer Evander Holyfield's heart? What did Holyfield himself have to say about his healing?

2. What error commonly occurs on the part of those relating so-called miraculous healings, such as what happened to Heidi? What does this tell us about the credibility level of nearly all reported accounts of healing miracles? What additional factors contribute to inaccuracies in reported miraculous healings?

3. How much hard evidence typically accompanies reports of healing miracles? What has been the author's experience when he has tried to substantiate the evidence for such miracles?

CHAPTER 6
HOW COMMON ARE GENUINE
MIRACLES OF HEALING?

1. What did the author conclude about the miracle healing of baby Iyanna? Why did he come to that conclusion?

2. What lesson is to be learned from the Catholic Church's monitoring of the reputed miraculous healings at the shrine at Lourdes?

3. How many miracles of physical healing has the author personally observed? How many have the famous physicians Paul Brand and C. Everett Koop—former surgeon general of the United States—observed?

4. What are we to conclude about the frequency of healing miracles from the mass of evidence examined in this book? What do you believe about healing miracles happening today? Have you ever experienced a healing miracle? If so, have you subjected it to a process of thorough investigation?

5. Does the infrequency of miraculous healings today mean God has ceased to work supernaturally in the world? If God continues to work supernaturally in the world today, how does he do it? In your opinion, are spiritual miracles any less miraculous than physical miracles?

Chapter 7
Solomon's Clues

1. Why does the author say he spent so much time in this book trying to arrive at the true definition and frequency of physical miracles? What personal connection does the author have to these issues? Have you or someone you know ever experienced a loved one who prayed for healing and didn't receive it?

2. What's so wrong with a little exaggeration about the frequency of miraculous healings? How do wrong ideas about miracle healings affect our "God mosaic"?

3. If you had a loved one with a severe physical illness, how would you pray for his or her healing? How would you encourage him or her to pray? What would you tell him or her about the possibility of a miraculous healing from God?

A FURTHER EXAMINATION OF SCRIPTURE: DOES GOD PROMISE US PERFECT HEALTH?

In chapter 4, "What Do You Think, Doc?" we examined what God tells us in the Bible on the subject of healing and miracles. The section below will take a look at verses that are taken out of context by faith healers to "prove" their erroneous theology. And I am going to show you a response to every one of them based on a careful examination of Scripture.

NONE OF THE DISEASES?

> He said, "If you listen carefully to the voice of the LORD your God and do what is right in his eyes, if you pay attention to his commands and keep all his decrees, I will not bring on you any of the diseases I brought on the Egyptians, for I am the LORD, who heals you." (Ex. 15:26)

Whenever you're trying to interpret a verse, always ask, Who is being addressed? In this particular verse, God is speaking directly to the children of Israel. In God's divine parenting strategy, he was offering the children of Israel a reward for obeying his commands—sort of like a doctor rewarding a child with a lollipop for good behavior. It was also part of the covenant made specifically with Israel that outlined health and prosperity in exchange for obedience.

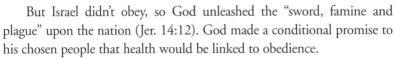

But Israel didn't obey, so God unleashed the "sword, famine and plague" upon the nation (Jer. 14:12). God made a conditional promise to his chosen people that health would be linked to obedience.

This promise has never been made to the New Testament church.

JESUS CHRIST THE SAME ...

Some quote the verse, "Jesus Christ is the same yesterday and today and forever" (Heb. 13:8) to support their argument that if Christ did miracles in the past, then the Trinity is doing the same miracles today.

But we've already discussed this and proved this line of thinking wrong in other books of this series. God's *nature* never changes, but his *actions* do based on his wisdom in parenting mankind. Henry W. Frost, in his book *Miraculous Healing*, points out that the Old Testament records only about fifty miracles, spread out over a period of approximately four thousand years. Of this number, only three involved miraculous healing of a physical nature (with the exception of the children of Israel looking upon the serpent for healing). Almost all of the miracles recorded in the Old Testament were miracles of nature.[1]

Now contrast this with the New Testament. Most of the miracles recorded were miracles of physical healing, and very few had to do with miracles of nature. All of Christ's miracles were crammed into a time span of only three and a half years, just before he died at about the age of thirty-three. Wasn't Jesus Christ the "same" at age twenty-one as he was at thirty-one? Then why didn't he do miracles at a younger age? And wasn't Jesus Christ the same when he existed as a member of the Trinity even before Abraham was born? (John 8:58). Jesus Christ has been present everywhere since the beginning of time. So why don't we see recorded in the Old Testament hundreds of miracles of physical healing like those seen in the New Testament? If we use the logic in the argument presented above, then Christ wasn't the same because he didn't do miracles earlier in his life, nor did he perform the same miracles earlier in history; therefore, Hebrews 13:8 must be a lie if we use the logic presented in the faith healer's argument.

DOES GOD STILL DO MIRACLES?

Throughout the Scriptures we see different types of miracles performed in select periods by select individuals for select purposes. In the Old Testament it was mainly miracles of nature. In the New Testament it was mainly miracles of physical healing. Today (as pointed out earlier in this book) almost all the miracles we see are of a spiritual nature with the miraculous spiritual conversion of millions of people. God's *nature* never changes, but he does choose to *work* differently at different periods.

To argue that the parenting strategies of God the Father and Jesus Christ the Son are the same, or should be the same, today as they were two thousand or four thousand years ago means that we should be following a pillar of cloud by day, a pillar of fire by night, gathering manna for food, raising our hands to try and make the sun stand still, while living in constant fear that God will strike us dead on the spot for telling a single lie—as he did with Ananias and Sapphira as recorded in the New Testament (Acts 5:1–11).

ALL YOUR DISEASES?

> Praise the LORD, O my soul; all my inmost being, praise his
> holy name. Praise the LORD, O my soul, and forget not all his
> benefits—who forgives all your sins and heals all your diseases.
> (Ps. 103:1–3)

King David, his heart bursting with joyous praise for his Maker, penned this beautiful psalm of God's goodness in the context of God's unique covenant relationship with Israel as discussed above. God's benefits to the nation included: forgiveness of sins (v. 3), healing of diseases (v. 3), deliverance from death (v. 4), and satisfaction of desires (v. 5). When David acknowledged that God "heals all your diseases," he was simply giving God the credit and the glory for every healing. David wasn't talking to believers today, saying, "God promises to instantly heal every single disease you will ever acquire." The psalmist was saying that when you are healed, healing comes from God.

This fits perfectly with what God says to Israel in Deuteronomy 32:39:

> See now that I myself am He! There is no god besides me. I put to death and I bring to life, I have wounded and I will heal, and no one can deliver out of my hand.

Remember what God said to Moses:

> The LORD said to him, "Who gave man his mouth? Who makes him deaf or mute? Who gives him sight or makes him blind? Is it not I, the LORD?" (Ex. 4:11)

God is saying, "People of Israel, I—and only I—am the sovereign God of the universe! Death, life, sickness, protection, and health lie exclusively in my hand. If you die, or are sick, I allowed it. If you are healed, I am responsible for the healing—*all* healing. Nothing happens in the game of life over which I do not have complete control."

Did God heal every one of David's diseases? He could have if he wanted—but he didn't. David's "bones wasted away," and his "strength was sapped" due to his guilt (Ps. 32:3–4). David eventually did recover. However, in the end, David—like every other saint apart from Enoch and Elijah—died, was buried, and his body decayed (Acts 13:36).

HOW LONG DOES GOD GIVE US?

> The length of our days is seventy years—or eighty, if we have the strength. (Ps. 90:10)

How do some faith healers explain away the aging process and the worldwide phenomenon of death in relation to "God's promise to heal"? Some claim that God promises us perfect health up to seventy or eighty years of age, then he will allow us to die. And they use the first half of Psalm 90:10 as the proof.

Taking a close look, though, at the *full* verse in context, we see the true meaning:

> You have set our iniquities before you, our secret sins in the light of your presence. All our days pass away under your wrath; we finish our years with a moan. The length of our days

DOES GOD STILL DO MIRACLES?

is seventy years—or eighty, if we have the strength; yet their span is but trouble and sorrow, for they quickly pass, and we fly away. Who knows the power of your anger? For your wrath is as great as the fear that is due you. Teach us to number our days aright, that we may gain a heart of wisdom. (Ps. 90:8–12)

The context here is speaking of God's wrath on all of mankind for his sin; absolutely nothing here indicates a promise to keep us healthy till seventy or eighty years of age. The second half of Psalm 90:10 reads, "Yet their span is but trouble and sorrow." God will keep us healthy until seventy or eighty years of age, but our "span is but trouble and sorrow"? It just doesn't make sense. This is another example of a verse (half a verse actually) being wrenched from its context to try and prove the deceitful "health and wealth" gospel.

Furthermore, consider this: The average life span at the turn of the twentieth century in America was about forty-seven years. Millions of godly men and women in the past couple of centuries in particular—including some prominent faith healers—have died before their seventieth birthday.

Where is God's promise in the Scriptures to keep believers healthy till seventy years of age?

There is no such promise.

CONTINUING SIGNS AND WONDERS?

You performed miraculous signs and wonders in Egypt and have continued them to this day, both in Israel and among all mankind, and have gained the renown that is still yours. (Jer. 32:20)

Some believe that Jeremiah was declaring that God was commonly performing these miraculous signs and wonders worldwide "to this day." They would argue that this is proof that signs and wonders were commonplace "among all mankind"

No evidence elsewhere in Scripture indicates that miraculous signs and wonders were common and pervasive throughout the entire Old Testament period of history—not in the land of Israel, and not in any other part of the world. The signs and wonders mentioned here refer to the unique supernatural events that took place in Egypt (i.e., the plagues) that brought about the deliverance of the children of Israel from bondage (Jer. 32:21; see also Deut. 4:34).

John Calvin explains the particular phrase "to this day" as meaning "*memorable* even unto this day."[2] Not only would Israel remember this great deliverance in the Passover memorial every year, but these signs and wonders that God performed in Egypt would also cause neighboring nations to remember God's great name "to this day"—specifically his power, justice, and wrath (Ex. 9:16; 1 Chron. 17:21; Isa. 63:12). Many commentators interpret the verse this way.

Others believe Jeremiah was stating that God continued to perform other signs and wonders in Israel up until Jeremiah's day—however, only sporadically and in the presence of certain leaders. Both of these views would fit with what we know to be true about Israel and Old Testament history as a whole.

What cannot be argued from this verse is that miraculous signs and wonders were frequently being performed all around the world.

SET FREE?

Because through Christ Jesus the law of the Spirit of life set me free from the law of sin and death. (Rom. 8:2)

Some interpret this verse to mean that we, as true believers, are set free from the *physical* curse of the law of sin and death, meaning that we are free from all manner of sickness and disease. But from the context, Paul is not talking about the physical laws but rather the *spiritual* laws of sin and death. Paul clarifies the meaning of verse 2 in verse 10 of the same chapter: "But if Christ is in you, your body is dead because of sin, yet your spirit is alive because of righteousness." Paul contrasts this statement with, "What a wretched man I am! Who will rescue me from this body of death?" (Rom. 7:24). He's saying that we are set free from the bondage of our sin nature and eternal death—*not physical death.* "Who will rescue me from this body of death?" If Christ were to literally set us free from the physical effects of the law of sin and death, then no believer would age, become sick, or die. Obviously this is not the case. Again, you cannot separate the disease process from the physical process of aging and death.

Christ will one day set us completely free from our mortal body of death and redeem our perishable bodies—but not until the final day of redemption (Rom. 8:11, 23; 1 Cor. 15:42–44; Phil. 3:20–21; Rev. 21:4).

GREATER WORKS?

> "Truly, truly, I say to you, he who believes in Me, the works that I do, he will do also; and greater *works* than these he will do; because I go to the Father. (John 14:12 NASB)

The key question that immediately arises is, To whom is Jesus speaking here? Every believer? Some believers? Or just the disciples? An examination of the context reveals that Christ was speaking to the disciples. But was he also extrapolating his words to all believers?

To begin with, the word "works" from the phrase "greater works" is not in the original Greek manuscripts (that's why "works" is in italics in the KJV and NASB). The phrase "greater works" is translated "greater things" in the NIV, which, as R. V. G. Tasker and other commentators contend, is a more literal rendering, referring to the Greek *ergon*.[3]

Bible commentator Arthur W. Pink also points out that Christ says, "He *will* do even greater things than these." Christ didn't say he *might* do greater things than these.[4] But Paul asks the rhetorical question, "Are all apostles? Are all prophets? Are all teachers? Do all work miracles? Do all have gifts of healing?" (1 Cor. 12:29–30). If you argue that "greater things" means greater miracles, then you have two problems.

First, in New Testament history most believers did not perform the miraculous. So when Christ said you *will* do greater things, he had to have been emphatically speaking to the disciples who actually did the miraculous for a season (Matt. 10:1; 2 Cor. 12:12).

The *second* problem is this: If you argue that "greater things" refers to miracles, how were the disciples going to perform greater miracles

A FURTHER EXAMINATION OF SCRIPTURE

than Christ, who fed the five thousand, made the blind to see, and raised the dead back to life? How can you top these signs and wonders with "greater things"?

It becomes apparent that "greater things" doesn't mean greater in power, but greater in magnitude. The disciples collectively would spread the gospel to more and more distant places than Christ, and see more conversions than Christ did. For example, three thousand people were converted after hearing one sermon from Peter! Christ was reassuring his apostles here, that even though he would go away, he would send the counselor, the Holy Spirit (John 14:16), who would aid their efforts by supernaturally empowering them and convicting people of their sin.

William Hendriksen, in his commentary on John, says that Christ was referring more so to miracles in the spiritual realm, than those in the physical realm. "Greater works," says Hendriksen, are most likely connected "with *the conversion of the Gentiles.* Such works were of a higher character and vaster in extent."[5] (John 5:20–21; 12:23–32; 17:20).

Hendriksen makes the acute observation:

> The miracles in the physical realm are subservient to those in the spiritual sphere: the former serve to prove the genuine character of the latter. Does Jesus, perhaps, by means of this very comparison, which places the spiritual so far above the physical, hint that miracles in the physical sphere would gradually disappear when they would no longer be necessary?[6]

I have spent thousands of hours working in hospitals in the United States and Canada caring for some of the sickest and most disabled patients alive. Some patients are completely paralyzed from the neck down and will never walk again. Not once have I seen or heard of anyone with the gift of healing coming into a hospital and healing such a patient.

But Jesus and his disciples did.

John 14:12 cannot be used to argue that we will do greater miracles than Christ did two thousand years ago. What could possibly be greater than raising the dead? If you argue otherwise, where is the scriptural evidence and irrefutable tangible proof today?

It simply doesn't exist.

DOES GOD STILL DO MIRACLES?

ANOTHER FOUNDATION?

Am I saying that the foundational gifts (such as the gifts of healing and prophecy) seen in the early church will *never* reappear?

Not exactly. Joel prophesied that a day was coming when Israel's "sons and daughters will prophesy, your old men will dream dreams, your young men will see visions" (Joel 2:28). He further prophesied a few verses later that God "will show wonders in the heavens and on the earth, blood and fire and billows of smoke. The sun will be turned to darkness and the moon to blood before the coming of the *great and dreadful day of the* LORD" (vv. 30–31). Some believe that we are living in just that day, the "latter rains" spoken of by Joel, when God is showcasing these wonders all around us. Is this thinking correct?

Peter quoted these words from Joel in Acts 2:16–21. Some denominations have taken Peter to mean that the prophecy was totally fulfilled on the day of Pentecost (the birth of the church). This is incorrect, for we have yet to see the "blood and fire and billows of smoke," and we have yet to see the sun "turned to darkness" and the "moon to blood," which will all occur just before Christ returns. "Peter was simply telling those present at Pentecost that they were getting a preliminary glimpse, a projection of the kind of power that the Spirit would release in the millennial kingdom."[7]

Yes, there is a day coming when some will be prophesying, dreaming divine dreams, and seeing divine visions. But till that dreadful day of the Lord when there will be blood, fire, billows of smoke, and the darkening of the moon and sun with judgment, we need to be on our guard against the false teachings from false prophets (see Jer. 23:16–32). Don't venture blindly into these spiritual traps like gullible sheep; rather, walk surely as a wise believer with your trusted treasure map, "accurately handling the word of truth" (2 Tim. 2:15 NASB).[9]

APPENDIX 2
E-MAIL FROM A READER

I received the following e-mail from a reader who read a modified excerpt (taken from this book) in Focus on the Family's magazine *Physician* (March/April 2004).

Hello,

I would like to begin by saying that I appreciate Dr. Burke's concern for patients who might be misled by false claims of miraculous interventions.... I would like to point out, though, what I perceive to be a wrong way of thinking about this issue found in Dr. Burke's article. That is, the assumption that if a great miracle had occurred it would soon be broadcast on network TV. The Scriptures often times point out a different approach to healing. We see in the Gospels that often times Jesus was motivated to keep his miracles of healing a secret. Thus, we find him sending people out of the room when he raises a child from the dead. We often see him telling people not to tell anyone what he has done. In addition, we also see Elijah, Elisha, and Peter raising the dead behind closed doors. Paul raises the dead in the middle of the night. There are, to be sure, exceptions, but it is clear that many of the miracles performed in the Bible were not witnessed by the multitudes and were intended to be kept secret....

If God chose to heal someone without the assistance of doctors, no one could verify the miracle, because it had not been diagnosed by a medical expert. Yet the person would know if he or she had been healed, and the fact that the doctor did not have the medical tests to prove that sickness had been present would not in any way diminish the truthfulness of the claim to the miracle.

DOES GOD STILL DO MIRACLES?

I replied a short time later in an e-mail:

> Dear _____,
>
> Thank you very much for your e-mail. You have raised some good questions.
>
> You are right in saying that God does perform miracles of healing that are not always highly visible. You gave some examples from the NT that need to be examined in more detail.
>
> The passages regarding Jesus' healing of the blind men are interesting. In Matthew 9:27–30 Jesus told the blind men not to say anything, but they ran off and spread the news all over the region.
>
> In Mark 7:32–35 Jesus healed a man who was deaf and then told him not to tell anyone. But he did anyway.
>
> In John 9:1–7 Jesus healed another blind man who went out and told all the rulers.
>
> In Luke 7:12–15 Jesus healed a man right out of his coffin (the coffin was in a funeral procession).
>
> In Mark 2:3–12 Jesus healed a paralytic who was lowered through the roof in front of a large crowd.
>
> You are right when you say that there were many miracles performed that were kept secret. But as evidenced above, there were many miracles that were very public. There are many more examples of spectacular miracles in the NT that by today's standards would have made the headlines of major newspapers or been showcased on reputable TV networks. To my knowledge, there have never been any news stories in any credible newspaper or TV networks documenting a genuine miracle like those described above, where someone was raised from the dead, someone blind from birth had vision fully restored, or someone totally paralyzed had instantly regained normal strength.
>
> The point I'm trying to make is not that we should expect to see highly publicized evidence for every genuine miracle of healing that God performs (I'm sorry if it came across like this in the article), but that we should be seeing more evidence of miracles of healing on major news networks if God is still performing the same miracles of healing, on a similar scale, today as he did in Bible times. When was the last time

you saw on TV, or read in the newspaper, of someone having instant restoration of sight, strength, or life in someone totally blind, paralyzed, or dead? We are not seeing these miracles performed as the citizens did in Jesus' day. [Yet every time a Virgin Mary statue "weeps" the media is all over the news event.] Not every spectacular miracle of healing will make the evening news, but why have we not seen even one?...

You also remarked that doctors may not always have a chance to examine a patient before the miracle takes place. In North America, nearly everyone with a severe disease or disorder has seen at least one medical doctor who could verify a genuine miracle of healing if it later occurred. Anyone with blindness, deafness, or spinal-cord paralysis has seen at least one doctor who could attest to a miracle.

I know you didn't directly raise this issue, but a medical doctor doesn't need to see the actual transformation before his or her eyes. Currently, I am working in one of the largest spinal-cord rehab centers in Canada. If I see one of my spinal-cord injured patients one day who is completely paralyzed from the neck down, with contractures, muscle atrophy, skin ulcers, and spasticity, and the next day that patient comes in running and jumping around, with normal muscle bulk, tone, and strength, I would label this a genuine miracle. I don't need to actually see the event to believe it is a true miracle, because there is no medical explanation whatsoever for such an event. But again, no reputable news network or newspaper has ever documented such a miracle. This would be very easy to do. All it would involve is the patient going back to see his or her doctor—just like those healed of leprosy went back to the priests to confirm that they were healed. The fact that we are not seeing the same types of miracles, on the same scale as in Jesus' day gives us a clue that something has changed. I believe that God is still performing miracles of physical healing today, but for the most part these are very rare.

It all cascades back to the question, What was the purpose of miracles in the Bible?

Again, thanks for your e-mail. If you would like to discuss the topic more, feel free to drop me another e-mail.

Sincerely,
Brad Burke, MD

NOTES

INTRODUCTION

1. David Connuck, et al., "Incidence of Patent Ductus Arteriosus and Patent Foramen Ovale in Normal Infants," *The American Journal of Cardiology* 89 (January 15, 2002): 244–47.

2. How did I know this "hole" was a patent ductus arteriosus and not an actual hole in the aorta? Three reasons: 1) Patent ductus arteriosus is a fairly common disorder, initially treated with medications (some adults still have a very tiny, insignificant patent ductus); 2) if it was an actual hole in the aorta, the child would have bled into her chest and would have been dead within minutes; 3) doctors don't wait around for days, giving a child medications to try and fix life-threatening aortic ruptures or dissections. Surgery is instituted immediately. I also sent a letter to the renowned pastor of this church regarding the service that Sunday. His assistant left a message on my answering machine to call and speak with him. When I called he wasn't available to speak with me, and he never returned my phone call.

3. Kenneth L. Woodward, et al., "What Miracles Mean," *Newsweek*, May 1, 2000, 54, adapted from Kenneth L. Woodward, *The Book of Miracles* (New York: Simon & Schuster, 2000).

4. John MacArthur, *The Power of Suffering: Strengthening Your Faith in the Refiner's Fire* (Wheaton, IL: Victor Books, 1995).

5. Ibid.

6. Ibid.

7. Dr. Paul Brand, personal letter, March 14, 2003.

8. John F. MacArthur, Jr., *Charismatic Chaos* (Grand Rapids, MI: Zondervan, 1992), 127–28.

CHAPTER 1
THE GREATEST MIRACLE WORKER

1. Peter Jennings, "Poll on Importance of Religion in America," *World News Tonight with Peter Jennings*, ABC, March 28, 1997.

2. Loren Haarsma, "Why believe in a creator?: Perspectives on Evolution," *The World & I* 11 (January 1, 1996): 322.

3. C. S. Lewis, *Miracles* (New York: Touchstone [Simon & Schuster], 1996), 220.

4. John F. MacArthur, Jr., *Charismatic Chaos* (Grand Rapids, MI: Zondervan, 1992), 146.

5. "Now Jesus himself was about thirty years old when he began his

NOTES

ministry…. (Luke 3:23). Dr Harold Hoehner (a Dallas Theological Seminary professor with a PhD from Cambridge) in his book *Chronological Aspects of the Life of Christ* (Grand Rapids, MI: Zondervan, 1977), page 43, concludes that "the birth of Christ occurred either in December, 5 BC, or January, 4 BC …" On page 44 Hoehner continues, "Therefore, it is concluded that Christ's ministry began sometime in the summer or autumn of AD 29." Therefore, according to Dr. Hoehner, Jesus was approximately 32.5 when he began his ministry. (Don't forget that 1 BC is followed by AD 1) Luke says Christ was "about thirty years old" when he began his ministry, so 32.5 is quite reasonable.

Now we know that Jesus' ministry started just *after* he was baptized (Luke 3:21–23). Crossing over to John's gospel 1:32 John says "I saw" Jesus' baptism. The verb "saw" is in the perfect tense that describes an action that was completed in the past. "The next day" (John 1:35) and the second "next day" (John 1:43) preceed the "third day" that begins the story in Cana beginning in John 2:1. Therefore, we can stand in confidence on the Word of God that Christ's first miracle performed at Cana (John 2:11) was *after* his baptism—the beginning of his ministry—when Christ was about 30 years old, perhaps as old as 32.5 according to Dr. Harold Hoehner.

6. *Decision*, April 2003, http://www.billygraham.org/ourMinistries/decision Magazine/ article.asp?i=310 (accessed June 2004).

7. As quoted by A. Duane Litfin, "1 Timothy," in John F. Walvoord, Roy B. Zuck, eds., *The Bible Knowledge Commentary: An exposition of the Scriptures by Dallas Seminary Faculty,*

New Testament Ed. (Wheaton, IL: Victor Books, 1983), 733.

8. MacArthur, *Charismatic Chaos,* 127–28.

CHAPTER 2
FAITH HEALERS: GOD'S SERVANTS OR GOD'S EMBARRASSMENTS?

1. Sinikka Kahl, "A Place to Feel at Home: Africa's Independent Churches," *The World & I* 10 (December 1, 1995): 194.

2. James Randi, *The Faith Healers* (Buffalo: Prometheus Books, 1987), 141–42, 150.

3. I observed this temporary use of wheelchairs in the Benny Hinn miracle crusade I attended. Dr. Nolen observed the same as documented in his book and discussed in this book.

4. Randi, *The Faith Healers*, 113–14.

5. Grant would angle the seated individual in such a way that exaggerated the leg length discrepancy to the audience. Then, realigning the person's legs, Grant would very cleverly slip the shoe gently away from the heel, making it appear as though the leg had lengthened. This trick worked the best with individuals wearing cowboy boots. Ibid., 128–29. (See also photographs pp. 166–67.)

6. Ibid., 104–5.

7. William A. Nolen, *Healing: A Doctor in Search of a Miracle* (New York: Random House, 1975), 208–11, 228–38.

8. As quoted in, "Charlatans in the Church," *U.S. News & World Report*, March 29, 1993, 51.

9. Admittedly, Satan is very powerful, and it is possible that he can perform

some extraordinary feats through certain people.

10. Benny Hinn, "Double Portion Anointing, Part # 3" audiotape #A031791-3 as cited by Hank Hanegraaff, *Christianity in Crisis* (Eugene, OR: Harvest House Publishers, 1993), 341.

11. Nolen, *Healing: A Doctor in Search of a Miracle*, 53–54.

12. Ibid., 48.

13. Ibid., 66.

14. Ibid., 65.

15. Ibid.

16. Ibid., 67.

17. Ibid., 66.

18. Ibid., 72.

19. For documentation of these five cases, see Nolen, *Healing: A Doctor in Search of a Miracle*, 75–90.

20. Ibid., 75–79.

21. Ibid., 79–81.

22. Ibid., 81–84.

23. Ibid., 84–87.

24. Ibid., 87–90.

25. Ibid., 93.

26. Ibid., 94–95.

27. Ibid., 95, 97.

28. Ibid., 97, 99.

29. Ibid., 63, 93–94.

30. Ibid., 99.

31. Ibid., 100–101.

32. Ibid., 99–100.

33. Ibid., 268.

34. Gayle White, "The Healer and the Champ: Crusader of 'miracles' evokes strong reaction," *The Atlanta Journal and Constitution*, July 9, 1994, E/06.

35. Hank Hanegraaff, *Christianity in Crisis* (Eugene, OR: Harvest House Publishers, 1993), 341.

36. Ibid.

37. As quoted in White, "The Healer and the Champ: Crusader of 'miracles' evokes strong reaction."

38. I recently contacted the *Christian Research Institute*. They replied in a letter (March 23, 2005) that, at the time of this writing, Hinn has not provided CRI with any documented evidence of miraculous healings since the three nonmiracle cases he submitted in 1992.

39. The production notes for HBO's *A Question of Miracles*, printed in my material possession, and quoted on the Web site, http://www.pfo.org/hinn-hbo.htm (accessed February 28, 2003).

40. July 15, 1998 as quoted by Mike Oppenheimer, president of Let Us Reason Ministries, founded in 1994 as an up-to-date apologetic resource center. See quote at http://www.letusreason.org/b.hinn1.htm. See the same quote at The Spirit of Things: 18 January 2004—Spiritually Incorrect—Religion and Satire (ABC Radio National [Australian Broadcasting Corporation]) http://www.abc.net.au/rn/relig/spirit/stories/s1009993.htm (accessed January 1, 2005).

41. As seen on "Do you believe in Miracles?" *The Fifth Estate*, CBS, November 3, 2004.

42. Art Levine, "Detectives for Christ," *U.S. News & World Report*, December 8, 1997, 71.

43. During the service, Hinn introduced to the audience some of these front-row friends.

44. It wasn't that God had instantly restored them from a frailness to well-nourished bodies either, because many were mildly or moderately overweight and wearing loose-fitting clothing. Had God instantly increased their weight, their clothing would have been tight—and they would have said they miraculously put on weight. But why would God make them overweight? Doesn't he know that being overweight is bad for one's health?

45. "Do You Believe in Miracles?" *The Fifth Estate.* See also, http://www.cbc.ca/fifth/main_miracles.html (accessed January 2, 2005).

46. Ibid.

47. A long-time security specialist on Hinn's ministry team (disguised on camera) said, "That screening process has one purpose: to keep the truly sick or disabled away from Benny Hinn.... Those people are never allowed near the stage."

48. Part of the interview was aired on November 3, 2004, "Do You Believe in Miracles?" *The Fifth Estate.* For the full interview, see http://www.cbc.ca/fifth/justin.pdf (accessed January 2, 2005).

49. Ibid.

50. Justin Peters says, "I've often wondered if Benny Hinn knows he's a fake or if he's just so self-deluded. I'm not sure. I think initially in his ministry, I think he may have begun with honourable intentions, but he has become intoxicated by the money. He's ... become intoxicated by the power. He yields an incredible power over people and I think for him, it's a real—it's a real rush. But yes, I do—I do think he sees himself as some type of a messiah figure." For the full interview, see http://www.cbc.ca/ fifth/justin.pdf (accessed January 2, 2005).

51. Randi, *The Faith Healers,* 277.

52. Ibid., 194–95.

53. To read these letters, see Randi, *The Faith Healers,* 145, 202–4, 220–22, 264–67.

54. Hank Hanegraaff, *Counterfeit Revival* (Dallas: Word, 1997), 36. Regarding the miraculous breast appearance: "The Hunters now admit that they do not have a shred of evidence to support this story."

55. The girl was *not* "totally incapacitated, paralyzed, and blind," as was reported. Also, the girl remained "legally blind" after the healing. Hank Hanegraaff, *Counterfeit Revival,* 59–60.

56. Dick Dewert, president of CJIL-TV, a Canadian Christian television station, once claimed he had a tooth miraculously turn to gold. But Dewart's long-time dentist, Dr. Jack Sherman, said it was no miracle because *he* put it there himself. Barry Shlacter, "All That Glitters is not Gold at Religious Revival in Texas," *The Arizona Republic,* January 9, 2000, A17. With regard to the "miraculous gold teeth" phenomenon, Teresa Watanabe writes, "Never mind that they can't seem to prove it; disregard the dental records that contradict some of their claims." In an example cited, the pastor, Rich Oliver of the Family Christian Center in Orangevale, California swears God gave him a gold crown. "Actually, dental records show his earthly dentist put in the crown on April 29, 1991." When Oliver was confronted, he replied, "I'd have to say I was absolutely wrong." One man remarked, "Of all the things going on—cancer, war, disease—God is busy changing fillings? That's the best he can do?" Teresa Watanabe, "God, the divine dentist?" *The Toronto Star,* February 20, 2000, 1.

57. A) "*Charisma,* a Christian magazine that covers the charismatic-Pentecostal scene, had a lab test of four samples, three collected from Ms. Machado's visits to Toronto [Toronto Airport Fellowship Church], Virginia, and Washington, D.C. and one from Ms. Heflin in Virginia. In each case, the 'gold' dust was found to be plastic, or plastic with a trace of aluminum." Kimberly Winston, "Gold Rush: Glitter like dust is latest proof of God's

presence, Pentecostals say," *The Dallas Morning News*, October 9, 1999, 1G. B) "At some Canadian and U.S. revivals, gold flakes materialized along with the gold teeth. A geochemist at the University of Toronto analyzed such a bit and found it to be gold-colored glitter, made of plastic film. A gold speck found at a Dallas revival melted when heated, said Ole Anthony of the Trinity Foundation, a nonprofit organization that investigates alleged excesses by televangelists." Barry Shlacter, "All that glitters is not gold at religious revival in Texas," *The Arizona Republic*, January 9, 2000, A17.

58. Nolen, *Healing: A Doctor in search of a Miracle*, 85–86.

59. Carol McGraw, "Faith in His Hands," *The Orange County Register*, December 5, 1995, E01. See also the HBO investigative report, *A Question of Miracles*, April 15, 2001. Mike Oppenheimer, president of Let Us Reason Ministry, personally visited Hinn's crusades and noticed that the sickest, including a paralyzed friend of his, were never healed: www.letusreason.org/b.hinn1.htm (accessed January 1, 2005). Hank Hanegraaff has also attended Hinn's crusades, and writes, "Tragically, those who attended the meeting in wheelchairs ended up leaving in the same physical condition. Some departed in tears." Hanegraaff, *Christianity in Crisis*, 339.

60. We do not know for sure if Christ or the apostles miraculously healed patients with total severance of the spinal cord. In biblical times, such a person usually died shortly after the injury from bladder and kidney complications. However, Christ and his apostles could very well have miraculously healed spinal-cord injuries soon after the injury.

61. Benny Hinn, in his book *Welcome Holy Spirit*, bragged that he healed masses in the Sault Saint Marie, Ontario hospital. In the book it says, "After the service in the chapel, the Reverend Mother asked, "Oh, this is wonderful!! Would you mind coming now and laying hands on all the patients in the rooms who could not come to the services?" *The Fifth Estate* interviewed the nun who was the administrator of the hospital: "I did not do that. He did not ask me. And I did not do it. I wouldn't have done that." Benny Hinn also wrote, "People were under the power of the Holy Spirit up and down the hallways.... It was happening before my eyes. We were walking through a hospital and people were being healed." The nun replied, "No, no, no. That did not happen!" After sixty years as a nun, she says she does believe in miracles, but not what Benny said in his book. "Do You Believe in Miracles?" *The Fifth Estate*.

62. As quoted at http://www.thebelfast-berean.co.uk/Are%20the%20Miracles%20 Claims%20True.pdf (accessed January 1, 2005).

63. Nolen, *Healing: A Doctor in Search of a Miracle*, 84.

64. "Lourdes and Fatima Endorsed by Hinn," (*Personal Freedom Outreach*, 1998) http://www.pfo.org/endorsed.htm (accessed January 1, 2005).

65. These Bible studies were intended for people in the entertainment industry and everyone else was discouraged from attending. Though I was working as a doctor at the time, I was also writing full-length film screenplays, meeting with producers and entertainment lawyers, and having my work read by producers and other professionals in the film industry. I wrote three screenplays in total, one

of which was later optioned by an entertainment lawyer. Therefore, I felt that I had a legitimate basis to attend the Hollywood Bible study.

CHAPTER 3
INSIGHTS FROM THE WORLD OF MEDICINE

1. Herbert Benson, MD (with Marg Stark), *Timeless Healing: The Power and Biology of Belief* (New York: Simon & Schuster, 1996), 69.
2. M. E. McCullough, et al., "Religious involvement and mortality: a meta-analytic review," *Health Psychology* 19 (2000): 211–22.
3. H. G. Koenig, et al., "The relationship between religious activities and blood pressure in older adults," *International Journal of Psychiatry in Medicine* 28 (1998): 189–213.
4. Jennifer M. Aviles, MD, et al., "Intercessory Prayer and Cardiovascular Disease Progression in a Coronary Care Unit Population: A Randomized Controlled Trial," *Mayo Clinic Proceedings,* Mayo Clinic 76 (December 2001): 1192–98.
5. Pamela S. Chally, and Joan M. Carlson, "Spirituality, Rehabilitation, and Aging: A Literature Review," *Archives of Physical Medicine and Rehabilitation* 85 (July 2004). For more information on the subject, see Harold G. Koenig, MD, "Religion and Medicine IV: Religion, Physical Health, and Clinical Implications," *International Journal of Psychiatry in Medicine* 31(2001): 321–36.
6. Benson, *Timeless Healing,* 228–89.
7. Michele Lesie, "Studies find validity in faith's healing power/Religion good for health, scientists say," *Minneapolis Star Tribune,* November 28, 1998, 07B.
8. For example, J. Kabat-Zinn, et al, "Influence of a mindfulness meditation-based stress reduction intervention on rates of skin clearing in patients with moderate to severe psoriasis undergoing phototherapy (UVB) and photochemotherapy (PUVA)," *Psychosomatic Medicine* 60 (1998): 625–32.
9. Benson, *Timeless Healing,* 168.
10. Toshihiko Maruta, MD, et al., "Optimists vs Pessimists: Survival Rate Among Medical Patients Over a 30-Year Period," *Mayo Clinic Proceedings,* Mayo Clinic 75 (2000): 140–43.
11. Melanie Cooper-Effa, MD, et al., "Role of Spirituality in Patients with Sickle Cell Disease." *The Journal of the American Board of Family Practice* 14 (2001): 116–22. "This study shows an association of spiritual well-being with better perception of life control for patients with sickle cell disease. While the association exists for both existential and religious well-being, the association with existential well-being is stronger.... One can infer from this study, however, that the association found in past studies between disease outcome and quality of life with spirituality might be influenced more by existential well-being."
12. Vince Rause, "Quest for the Divine," *Los Angeles Time Magazine,* July 15, 2001; *Reader's Digest,* 160 (February 2002): 99–103. Citations to *Reader's Digest* edition.
13. Gayle White, "Religion: Mystery of healing: As believers proclaim the curative powers of prayer, many mainstream churches rediscover a tradition that sees the 'miraculous' as part of everyday life," *The Atlanta Journal and Constitution,* May 20, 1995, E/06.
14. Benson, *Timeless Healing,* 85.
15. S. R. Adler, "Refugee stress and folk

belief: Hmong sudden deaths," *Soc Sci Med* 40 (June 1995): 1623–29.

16. M. Vatta, et al., "Genetic and biophysical basis of sudden unexplained nocturnal death syndrome (SUNDS), a disease allelic to Brugada syndrome," *Hum Mol Genet* 11 (February 1, 2002): 337–45.

17. Adler, "Refugee stress and folk belief: Hmong sudden deaths," 1623–29.

18. Bernie S. Siegel, MD, *Love, Medicine & Miracles* (New York: Harper & Row, 1988), 35.

19. Benson, *Timeless Healing,* 31. Benson comes to this conclusion based on his own research as well as that of Dr. Alan H. Roberts et al., "The Power of Nonspecific Effects in Healing: Implications for Psychosocial and Biological Treatments," *Clinical Psychology Review* 13 (1993): 375–91, and J. A. Turner, et al., "The Importance of Placebo Effects in Pain Treatment and Research," *Journal of the American Medical Association* 271 (1994): 1609–14.

20. B. C. Tilley, et al., "Minocycline in rheumatoid arthritis. A 48-week, double-blind, placebo-controlled trial. MIRA Trial Group," *Annals of Internal Medicine* 122 (January 15, 1995): 81–89.

21. As quoted in Siegel, *Love, Medicine & Miracles,* 202.

22. S. L. Assefi, and M. Garry, "Absolute memory distortions: alcohol placebos influence the misinformation effect," *Psychological Science* 14 (January 2003): 77–80.

23. Dr. Granger believes that about half to three-fourths of the illness we see "originate in problems of the spirit rather than in breakdowns of the body" as paraphrased in Siegel, *Love, Medicine & Miracles,* 204.

24. Dr. Benson says, "Other studies indicate that between 60 and 90 percent of all our population's visits to doctors' offices are stress-related." In Benson, *Timeless Healing,* 49.

25. For example, Kroenke and Mangelsdorff followed up on fourteen common symptoms in an internal medicine clinic. Sixteen percent of the cases (that had at least one of these symptoms) were thought to have an organic cause, while 10 percent were labeled "psychologic," and 74 percent were of unknown etiology. The authors state, "It is probable that many of the symptoms of unknown etiology were related to psychosocial factors." Kurt Kroenke, MD, and David Mangelsdorff, MD, "Common Symptoms in Ambulatory Care: Incidence, Evaluation, Therapy, and Outcome," *The American Journal of Medicine* 86 (March 1989): 262–66.

26. Benson, *Timeless Healing,* 69.

27. For more information, see D. D. Price, "Psychological and neural mechanisms of the affective dimension of pain," *Science* 288 (June 9, 2000): 1769–72.

28. R. Dubner and K. Ren, "Endogenous mechanisms of sensory modulation," *Pain,* August 1999, S45–53.

29. H. L. Fields, "Pain modulation: expectation, opioid analgesia and virtual pain." *Progress in Brain Research* 122 (2000): 245–53.

30. J. M. Besson, "The neurobiology of pain," *Lancet* 353 (1999): 1610–15.

31. Ibid.

32. M. O. Urban and G. F. Gebhart, "Central mechanisms in pain," *The Medical Clinics of North America* 83 (May 1999): 585–96.

33. Urban and Gebhart, "Central mechanisms in pain," 585–96.

34. P. Rainville, M. C. Bushnell, and G. H. Duncan, "Representation of acute and

persistent pain in the human CNS: potential implications for chemical intolerance," *Annals of the New York Academy of Sciences* 933 (2001): 130–41.

35. F. J. Keefe, et al., "Pain and emotion: new research directions," *Journal of Clinical Psychology* 57 (April 2001): 587–607.

36. C. Villemure and M. C. Bushnell, "Cognitive modulation of pain: how do attention and emotion influence pain processing?" *Pain,* February 2002, 195–99.

37. Brian Vastag, "Scientists Find Connections in the Brain Between Physical and Emotional Pain," *The Journal of the American Medical Association* 290 (November 12, 2003).

38. See Dr. Stahl's comments in Vastag, "Scientists Find Connections in the Brain Between Physical and Emotional Pain."

39. There is also a secondary gain of monetary compensation in many workmen's compensation claims. Whether the patient is conscious of it or not, improvement in a patient's condition is frequently contingent on the legal status of a claim.

40. K. Ren and R. Dubner, "Central nervous system plasticity and persistent pain," *Journal of Orofacial Pain* 13 (1999): 155–63, discussion 164–71.

41. Urban and Gebhart, "Central mechanisms in pain."

42. H. P. Rome Jr. and J. D. Rome, "Limbically Augmented Pain Syndrome (LAPS): Kindling, Corticolimbic Sensitization, and the Convergence of Affective and Sensory Symptoms in Chronic Pain Disorders," *Pain Medicine* 1 (2000): 7–23.

43. I. G. Rashbaum and J. E. Sarno. "Psychosomatic concepts in chronic pain," *Archives of Physical Medicine and Rehabilitation* 84 (2003): S76–80.

44. "Prospective studies, however, now show that emotional disturbance is also a significant risk factor for coronary artery disease and especially in those with pre-existing disease." C. Tennant and L. McLean, "The impact of emotions on coronary heart disease risk," *Journal of Cardiovascular Risk* 8 (June 2001): 175–83.

45. While these last two groups of individuals likely attend faith-healing services, I'm convinced they make up only a very small percentage of the audience.

46. "Recent neurological studies have shown that certain areas of the brain are stimulated by faith healers during their crusades. Their commanding speeches combined with music, the powerful psychological energy of large crowds focused on a single purpose, performing rituals in unison and susceptibility to hypnotic suggestion, can set off a chemical chain reaction in the brain that contributes to feelings of euphoria and an ability to break through pain barriers, at least temporarily." Production notes, "A Question of Miracles."

47. P. Rainville, "Dissociation of sensory and affective dimensions of pain using hypnotic modulation," *Pain,* August 1999, 159–71.

48. H. Sutcher, "Hypnosis as adjunctive therapy for multiple sclerosis: a progress report," *The American Journal of Clinical Hypnosis* 39 (April 1997): 283–90.

49. J. R. Dane, "Hypnosis for pain and neuromuscular rehabilitation with multiple sclerosis: case summary, literature review, and analysis of outcomes," *The International Journal of Clinical and Experimental Hypnosis* 44 (July 1996): 208–31.

50. Nolen, *Healing: A Doctor in Search of a Miracle*, 290.
51. Ibid., 82–83, 94.
52. Ibid., 91.
53. MacArthur, *Charismatic Chaos*, 127–28.
54. Nolen, *Healing: A Doctor in Search of a Miracle,* 101.
55. As quoted by Mike Oppenheimer in http://www.letusreason.org/b.hinn1.htm (accessed January 1, 2005).
56. C. Everett Koop, MD, hired an investigative writer who found such tactics used in healing campaigns. C. Everett Koop, MD, "Faith-Healing and the Sovereignty of God," in Michael Horton ed., *The Agony of Deceit* (Chicago: Moody Press, 1990), 179.

CHAPTER 4
"WHAT DO YOU THINK, DOC?"

1. As quoted in Richard Mayhue, *Divine Healing Today* (Chicago: Moody Press, 1983), 127–28.
2. As quoted in "Lourdes and Fatima Endorsed by Hinn," (*Personal Freedom Outreach*, 1998), http://www.pfo.org/endorsed.htm (accessed January 1, 2005).
3. Air Canada Centre, Toronto, Ontario, Canada, August 19, 2004.
4. W. E. Vine, Merrill F. Unger, and William White, *Vine's complete expository dictionary of Old and New Testament words* (Nashville: Thomas Nelson, 1996), Logos e-book, Vol. 2, 28.
5. Roger M. Raymer, "1 Peter," John F. Walvoord, Roy B. Zuck, eds., *The Bible Knowledge Commentary: An exposition of the Scriptures by Dallas Seminary Faculty, New Testament Ed.* (Wheaton, IL: Victor Books, 1983), 848.
6. Mayhue, *Divine Healing Today,* 51.
7. Paul C. Reisser, MD, "Healing: A Command Performance," *Physician,* May/June 2002, 22 (italics his).
8. John MacArthur Jr., *The MacArthur Study Bible*, electronic ed. (Nashville: Word, 1997), Logos e-book, (John 16:26–28).
9. The "name it and claim it" theology grossly contradicts Scripture (see Gen. 15:13; 50:20; Job 1 and 2; Ps. 119:67, 71, 75; Jer. 15:15; Mark 10:30; John 15:18–20; 16:2; Acts 22:4; Rom. 8:18–23; Heb. 11:35–38; 12:4–11; Rev. 2:8–11).
10. Kenneth E. Hagin, *Exceedingly Growing Faith* (Tulsa: Faith Library, 1983), 10 as quoted in MacArthur, *Charismatic Chaos,* 349.
11. Hagin, "How Jesus Obtained His Name" (Tulsa, OK: Rehma), tape #44H01 as quoted in MacArthur, *Charismatic Chaos,* 349.
12. Admittedly, it is possible that this "thorn" was not sickness. Nevertheless, whatever this "thorn" was, it was causing Paul some grief and suffering.
13. Frederick K. C. Price, *Is Healing for All?* (Tulsa, OK: Harrison House, 1976), 20, as quoted in Hanegraaff, *Christianity in Crisis*, 237.
14. Hank Hanegraaff, "Sickness, Suffering, and the Sovereignty of God," tape # C173, 2000.
15. Hanegraaff, *Christianity in Crisis, 237.*
16. Hagin, *Classic Sermons*, Word of Faith 25th Anniversary 1968–1992 (Tulsa, OK: Kenneth Hagin Ministries, 1992), 159, as quoted in Hanegraaff, *Christianity in Crisis,* 237.
17. Hanegraaff, *Christianity in Crisis, 237.* For extensive documentation of these heart-crisis episodes Hagin suffered in 1939, 1942, 1949, and 1973 see pages 402–3. Interestingly enough, in 1979 Hagin wrote a book in which he said,

"I have not had one sick day in 45 years": *The Name of Jesus* (Tulsa, OK: Kenneth Hagin Ministries, 1979), 133, as quoted in Hanegraaff, *Christianity in Crisis,* 401.

18. Gretchen Passantino, "Kenneth Hagin Sr., Father of Word-Faith Movement, Dies," *Christian Research Journal* 26 (2003): 53.

19. Randi, *The Faith Healers,* 65.

20. Hanegraaff, *Christianity in Crisis,* 238.

21. Randi, *The Faith Healers,* 88.

22. John MacArthur, "Charismatic Chaos: Does God still heal?" tape GC #90–60, 1991.

23. John Wimber, *Power Healing* (San Francisco: Harper & Row, 1987), xviii, as quoted in MacArthur, *Charismatic Chaos,* 240.

24. G. Richard Fisher, "Can You Be Deceived? Why People Are Duped and How Not to Be," http://www.pfo.org/deceived.htm (accessed January 1, 2005.)

25. Roberts Liardon, *John G. Lake: The Complete Collection of His Life Teachings* (Tulsa, OK: Albury Publishing, 1999), 13.

26. Ibid., 22.

27. Hanegraaff, "Sickness, Suffering, and the Sovereignty of God," tape # C173, 2000.

28. Robert S. Schwartz and David M. Buchner, "Exercise in the Elderly: Physiologic and Functional Effects," in *Principles of Geriatric Medicine and Gerontology,* 4th Ed., William R. Hazzard, MD et al eds. (New York: McGraw-Hill, 1999), 146.

29. Benson, *Timeless Healing,* 112.

30. Ibid., 114.

31. Henry W. Frost, *Miraculous Healing* (Great Britain: Christian Focus Publications with OMF Publishing, 1999).

32. C. J. Mansfield, J. Mitchell, and D. E. King, "The Doctor as God's mechanic? Beliefs in the Southeastern United States," *Social Science & Medicine* 54 (2002): 399–409.

33. Harold G. Koenig, Kenneth I. Pargament, and Julie Nielsen, "Religious Coping and Health Status in Medically Ill Hospitalized Older Adults," *The Journal of Nervous and Mental Disease* 186 (September 1998): 513–21.

34. Frost, *Miraculous Healing,* 37.

35. Ibid., 39.

36. As heard on Hank Hanegraaff's radio broadcast, "The Top 10 Outrages of 2002," CD #670 (Part B), 2003.

37. G. Subramanian, MD, et al., "Implications of the Human Genome for Understanding Human Biology and Medicine," *The Journal of the American Medical Association* 286 (November 14, 2001): 2296–307.

38. Admittedly, there are some inherited disorders where abnormal genes both "load the gun" *and* "pull the trigger."

39. Mayhue, *Divine Healing Today,* 127–28.

40. The succeeding verses in context (James 5:17–18) concern God's prophet Elijah: "Elijah was a man just like us." We sometimes get discouraged and morally weary in life, and Elijah, even though he was a chosen prophet of God, was no different. He became depressed over his lack of success and his enemies trying to kill him (1 Kings 19:4, 10). But he still prayed, and God answered his prayers. Looking at the context, this is further evidence that James is probably referring to spiritual discouragement rather than physical sickness.

41. J. Ronald Blue, "James," in John F. Walvoord, Roy B. Zuck, eds., *The Bible Knowledge Commentary: An exposition of the Scriptures by Dallas Seminary*

Faculty, New Testament Ed. (Wheaton, IL: Victor Books, 1983), 834.

42. Daniel R. Hayden, "Calling the Elders to Pray," *Bibliotheca Sacra* 138 (July/September 1981): 264.

43. It is worth pointing out that in all the healing miracles described in Acts, not once is the use of oil mentioned. Nor did Jesus use oil in his healing ministry.

44. Mayhue, *Divine Healing Today,* 66.

45. MacArthur, *Charismatic Chaos,* 208.

CHAPTER 5
"WHERE'S MY MIRACLE, LORD?"

1. Matthew W. Lively, DO, "Sports Medicine Approach to Low Back Pain," *The Southern Medical Journal* 95 (2002): 642–46. For a concise summary on the natural history (course) of acute low back (with studies cited), read this journal article.

2. Barry L. Beyerstein, "Social and Judgmental Biases That Make Inert Treatments Seem to Work," *Scientific Review of Alternative Medicine* 3 (1999): 20–33.

3. R. J. Papac, "Spontaneous regression of cancer: possible mechanisms," *In Vivo* 12 (November–December 1998): 571–78.

4. Larry Dossey, MD, *Healing Words: The Power of Prayer and the Practice of Medicine* (San Francisco: HarperSanFrancisco, 1993), 29, 242.

5. Koop, "Faith-Healing and the Sovereignty of God," 173.

6. Brad Burke, MD, "Looking for a Miracle," *Physician,* March/April 2004, 5–6.

7. Barbara LaDine, MD, "Retroactive Prayer?" *Physician,* July/August 2004, back cover.

8. After a modified excerpt of this chapter appeared in *Physician* magazine, I received an e-mail letter from a reader who felt that because Christ and the apostles often wanted their healings kept a secret, it would be wrong to expect a spectacular miracle to pop up in the media. To read this e-mail, along with my response, see appendix two, "E-mail from a reader."

9. "E Celebrity Profile [Hunter Tylo]," *Star Entertainment,* September 24, 2000, transcript unavailable.

10. Jeff Schultz, "Boxing: Misdiagnosis Linked to Post-Fight Drugs," *The Atlanta Journal and Constitution,* December 28, 1994, G/03.

11. Jeff Schultz, "Inside Boxing: Holyfield's doctor says 'stiff heart' was judgment call," *The Atlanta Journal and Constitution,* December 3, 1994, C/02.

12. Terence Moore, "Healthy or not, Holyfield should hang up gloves for good," *The Atlanta Journal and Constitution,* January 8, 1995, F/03.

13. Ron Williams, *Life's Highest Delight: Understanding the Person and Passion of God* (Cleveland, TN: Pathway Press, 1997), 43–46.

14. The author wrote that other miracles occurred: "As the doctors watched the dye in the CAT scan, pressure was suddenly released from her brain. Then the spleen, pancreas, lacerated liver, kidneys, and both sections of her broken pelvis were totally healed before an operation could be performed." First of all, a CAT scan is a snapshot of what the brain looks like, and you cannot see the pressure in the brain being "suddenly released" like a live picture on TV. Second, pancreatic lacerations are quite rare, and this report was probably an exaggeration. Third, in the majority of blunt trauma cases, bruised organs and fractured pelvises are not operated on.

They are most often treated conservatively and heal on their own. But even if this instantaneous healing actually happened, as the author noted, it leaves me to wonder why the doctors would afterward detail such a poor prognosis for the three-year-old? The facts in this case just don't add up.

15. It would appear that this story of healing from HIV is that of Linda Davies, whose audio testimony can be heard at http://www.healingrooms.com/swf/index.htm. She says in the audio message that her doctors told her the level of the virus was "undetectable" after retesting her. That doesn't necessarily mean she was completely healed. She didn't mention if she was on the usual drug cocktail that HIV patients take, which can lower the HIV levels to an undetectable level. She also didn't say that the doctors sent her home to die, but this was the message delivered in the video seminar—if she is the one they were referring to in the video seminar. (Web site accessed January 1, 2005.)

CHAPTER 6
HOW COMMON ARE GENUINE MIRACLES OF HEALING?

1. MacArthur, *Charismatic Chaos,* 153.
2. Official transcript of the show obtained from Burrelles Luce transcripts, PO Box 7, Livingston, NJ, 07039-0007 (http://www. BurrellesLuce.com/tt/ttothers.html).
3. Some skeptics might argue that the heartbeat was there all along, but that the doctors missed it. (There were at least two doctors present right from the beginning. Another pediatrician, Dr. Antoinette Sallamme, was also present and confirmed the events on Oprah's

show.). The chances of two (possibly more) experienced doctors failing to detect a heartbeat with a stethoscope and a monitor in a newborn are next to nil. Some might argue that the infant's heartbeat and breathing returned immediately after the doctors placed the infant in the mother's arms but that the mother didn't notice right away. Even if this did happen, the baby had been without a heartbeat for at least thirty minutes—possibly much longer (because they had no idea how long the child was pulseless in the womb). A child, surviving this length of time in a warm environment, without a heartbeat, with no residual effects, could still be considered a miracle.

4. Shereen El Feki, "Miracles Under the Microscope," *The Economist*, April 22, 2000, 85–87.
5. Woodward, et al., "What Miracles Mean," 54.
6. El Feki, "Miracles Under the Microscope."
7. Jason Horowitz, "Pope, Visiting Lourdes Shrine, Urges Compassion for the Sick," *New York Times,* August 15, 2004, 10.
8. Tim Blangger, "God is in the details: Many religious traditions include miracles as a matter of faith," *The Morning Call,* December 18, 2004, D9.
9. "Miracles Under the Microscope," *The Economist.* More recent articles (see Horowitz and Blangger above) report that the total number of miracles (sixty-six) remains the same. Therefore, to the best of my knowledge, still only four miracles have been accepted in more than four decades.
10. Randi, *The Faith Healers,* 20–30.
11. Woodward, et al., "What Miracles Mean."
12. Tim Blangger, "God is in the details:

Many religious traditions include miracles as a matter of faith."

13. Bob Ivry, "The Power of Prayer," *The Record* (Bergen County, NJ), March 28, 2004.
14. Philip Yancey, *Reaching for the Invisible God* (Grand Rapids, MI: Zondervan, 2000), 51–52.
15. Philip Yancey, *Soul Survivor: How My Faith Survived the Church* (New York: Doubleday, 2001), 65.
16. Ibid., 66.
17. Personal correspondence from Dr. Paul Brand, letter dated February 11, 2002.
18. As quoted in Philip Yancey, *Soul Survivor,* 184.
19. C. Everett Koop, MD, "Faith-Healing and the Sovereignty of God," in Michael Horton ed., *The Agony of Deceit,* 175.
20. James Dobson, *When God Doesn't Make Sense* (Wheaton, IL: Tyndale House Publishers, 1993), 109.
21. Charles R. Swindoll, *The Mystery of God's Will* (Nashville: W Publishing Group, 1999), 31.
22. John MacArthur, "Bible Questions and Answers," tape GC #70-19, 2000.
23. Hinn was referring here to physical miracles of healing. Air Canada Centre, Toronto, Ontario, Canada, August 19, 2004.
24. MacArthur, *Charismatic Chaos,* 153.
25. Christopher J. Mansfield, et al., "The Doctor as God's mechanic? Beliefs in the Southeastern United States."
26. Eighty percent of Americans in the southeast believe, either probably or most definitely, that "God acts through doctors to cure illness." Though these figures are not representative of the entire country, they would be fairly close to the national average. Mansfield et al., "The Doctor as God's mechanic? Beliefs in the Southeastern United States."
27. Dr. Paul Brand, personal letter to the author dated February 11, 2002.
28. Dr. Paul Brand, personal letter to the author dated March 14, 2003.
29. Siegel, *Love, Medicine & Miracles,* 34.
30. Air Canada Centre, Toronto, Ontario, Canada, August 19, 2004.
31. Dr. Paul Brand, personal letter to the author dated March 15, 2002.
32. Gordon D. Fee, *The Disease of the Health & Wealth Gospels* (Beverly, MA: Frontline Publishing, 1985), 31.

CHAPTER 7
SOLOMON'S CLUES

1. *Larry King Live,* August 17, 2001, CNN, http://www.cnn.com/TRAN-SCRIPTS/0108/17/lkl.00.html (accessed February 28, 2003.)
2. Hinn's own voice can be heard on Hank Hanegraaff's radio broadcast, *The Top 10 Outrages of 2002,* CD #670 (Part B), 2003. A guest on Hanegraaff's *Bible Answer Man* radio broadcast, Gretchen Passantino, points out that the man who was blind, whom Christ restored to perfect eyesight, didn't really know who Christ was. When questioned by the religious leaders, the man replied that this guy told him to go to Siloam and wash—and so he did. "He replied, 'Whether [Christ] is a sinner or not, I don't know. One thing I do know. I was blind but now I see!'" (John 9:25). The man didn't become blind again because he didn't believe in the person who healed him. In fact, it wasn't until much later that the man finally believed (John 9:35–38).
3. Hanegraaff, *Christianity in Crisis,* 261–62.
4. "Do you believe in Miracles?" *The Fifth Estate.*

5. *Good Morning America,* ABC, January 4, 2006.
6. www.healingrooms.com/iahr/iahr_leadership.htm (accessed June 15, 2004). He also writes on the same Web site, "Healing is the undergarment that God's army will wear to support the armor for battle." (I ask, where do we read this in the Bible?)
7. Koenig, Pargament, and Nielsen, "Religious Coping and Health Status in Medically Ill Hospitalized Older Adults," 513–21.
8. "My colleagues and I found that higher levels of negative religious coping were associated with poorer recovery of independence in activities of daily living in 96 medical rehabilitation patients followed over a four month period," says George Fitchett, http://www.ncracpe.org/Newsletters/May2001newsletter.pdf (accessed January 1, 2005). For his full study, see G. Fitchett, B. D. Rybarczyk, G. A. DeMarco, and J. J. Nicholas. "The role of religion in medical rehabilitation outcomes: a longitudinal study," *Rehabilitation Psychology* 44 (1999): 333–53.
9. Kenneth I. Pargament, et al., "Religious Struggle as a Predictor of Mortality among Medically Ill Elderly Patients: A Two Year-Longitudinal Study," *Archives of Internal Medicine* 161 (August 2001): 1881–85. The authors report that "the effects remained significant even after controlling for a number of possible confounding variables, including demographic, physical health, and mental health variables."
10. Kenneth I. Pargament, et al., "Religious Coping Methods as Predictors of Psychological, Physical and Spiritual Outcomes among Medically Ill Elderly Patients: A two-year Longitudinal Study," *Journal of Health Psychology* 9 (December 2004): 713–40.
11. James Dobson, *When God Doesn't Make Sense* (Wheaton, IL: Tyndale House Publishers, 1993), 14–15.
12. Air Canada Centre, Toronto, Ontario, Canada, August 19, 2004.

APPENDIX 1

1. Frost, *Miraculous Healing,* 88.
2. As quoted in A. R. Fausset, "Part Two Jeremiah-Malachi" in Jamieson, Robert, A. R. Fausset, David Brown, *A Commentary, critical, experimental, and practical, on the Old and New Testaments, Vol. 2* (Grand Rapids, MI: William B. Eerdmans, 1973), 113 (emphasis added).
3. R. V. G. Tasker, *The Gospel According to St. John: The Tyndale New Testament Commentaries* (Leicester, England: Inter-Varsity Press, 1960), 172.
4. Arthur W. Pink, *Exposition of the Gospel of John* (Grand Rapids, MI: Zondervan, 1975), 362.
5. William Hendriksen, *New Testament Commentary: Exposition of the Gospel According to John* (Grand Rapids, MI: Baker Books, 1953), 273.
6. Ibid.
7. MacArthur, *Charismatic Chaos,* 228.
8. J. Dwight Pentecost, *Things To Come: A Study in Biblical Eschatology* (Grand Rapids, MI: Zondervan, 1964), 230–31.
9. For a more detailed discussion on this question, see John F. MacArthur, Jr., *Charismatic Chaos,* 54–77, 287–89, and Stanley D. Toussaint's chapter "Acts," in John F. Walvoord, Roy B. Zuck, eds., *The Bible Knowledge Commentary: An Exposition of the Scriptures by Dallas Seminary Faculty, New Testament Ed.,* 358, 361–62.

Additional copies of *DOES GOD STILL DO MIRACLES?*
and other Victor titles
are available wherever good books are sold.

If you have enjoyed this book,
or if it has had an impact on your life,
we would like to hear from you.

Please contact us at:

VICTOR BOOKS
Cook Communications Ministries, Dept. 201
4050 Lee Vance View
Colorado Springs, CO 80918

Or visit our Web site:
www.cookministries.com

Victor®
The Bible Teacher's Teacher